CONTROLLED VIOLENCE

CONTROLLED VIOLENCE
ON THE FIELD
AND IN THE BOOTH

Sam Huff with Kristine Setting Clark

TRIUMPH
BOOKS

Library of Congress Cataloging-in-Publication Data

Huff, Sam.

 Controlled violence : on the field and in the booth / Sam Huff with Kristine Setting Clark.

  p. cm.

 Includes bibliographical references.

 ISBN 978-1-60078-518-4

1. Huff, Sam. 2. Football players—United States—Biography. 3. Sportscasters—United States—Biography. I. Clark, Kristine Setting, 1950– II. Title.

 GV939.H84C66 2011

 796.332092--dc22

 [B]

               2011013347

This book is available in quantity at special discounts for your group or organization.

For further information, contact:

Triumph Books

542 South Dearborn Street

Suite 750

Chicago, Illinois 60605

(312) 939–3330

Fax (312) 663–3557

www.triumphbooks.com

Printed in U.S.A.

ISBN: 978-1-60078-518-4

Design by Amy Carter

Photos courtesy of the author unless otherwise noted

To Patricia and Kevin from West Cork, Ireland.
You made this book possible.

You can run on a football field,
but you can't hide out there.

—Sam Huff

CONTENTS

FOREWORD

General Norman Schwarzkopf once said, "Sam Huff was what a linebacker is supposed to be: tough, aggressive, fast, and quick. Sam would make a great soldier. I'd be delighted to have him on my side."

But General Schwarzkopf didn't know Sam in his rookie year, when his career almost ended before it had begun. A tough lineman out of West Virginia, Huff came to the Giants' training camp in 1956, but didn't exactly impress the coaching staff.

Sam had just finished playing in the college all-star game only two days prior to training camp, so he was still pretty much bruised and sore. He didn't hit it off well with head coach Jim Lee Howell, who didn't take too kindly to rookies. None of the coaches could figure out which position he should play. Huff had mistaken an aging quarterback by the name of Charlie Conerly for a coach, then in his first exhibition game he hurt his knee. Fed up with coaches and training camp, he and fellow rookie Don Chandler decided to "run an out pattern" and hightail it back home, only to be talked out of quitting by an assistant coach named Vince Lombardi.

Sam returned to camp and beat the odds. Our defensive coach, Tom Landry, decided to try out Sam at what was then a new position, middle linebacker. It was as though the position had been made especially for him. With Landry's innovative 4-3 defense, Huff was a natural. As a matter of fact, he won the starting spot by the fourth week of the season and was the first rookie middle linebacker to start in an NFL championship game.

Huff had all the right qualities. At 6'1" and 230 pounds he not only possessed size and strength, but he was also mobile and fierce. He had a unique style of tackling—always aiming for the back shoulder. He never had a player cut back on him because he never allowed him the angle to do so. He hit with violence, and violence became his trademark.

Huff literally glamorized and brought notoriety to the position. He was the subject of a TV documentary—"The Violent World of Sam Huff"—that demonstrated to millions that the linebacker's world was a violent one.

Sam was relentless. He would stay on you and he would stay after you. The more threatened he felt, the more competitive he became. It's a confidence born of demonstrated ability. He thought he could will anything to happen on the field, and for the most part, it happened. Sam Huff played pro football with unmatched intensity, and he lived by one code: Get the man with the football.

—Frank Gifford, former New York Giants halfback
and Pro Football Hall of Fame member

FOREWORD

He was that rarity in professional football—an athlete who attained legendary status *during* his career.

Sam Huff was a coal miner's son from West Virginia. In 1956 he was drafted by the New York Giants as a defensive lineman, but when an assistant coach by the name of Tom Landry installed the revolutionary 4-3 defense he made Huff its anchor at middle linebacker.

In the spotlight of the world's media capital the New York defenders became heroes, and Huff was not only their leading man in this new, glamorous era of defensive football, but No. 70 was the first to bring notoriety to the position. He was a sought-after spokesman for advertisers and the first NFL player ever to be featured on the cover of *Time* magazine. He was even the star of a bold CBS documentary titled "The Violent World of Sam Huff." A linebacker has to be tough enough to play the run, graceful enough to play the pass, and mean enough to knock a runner out. Huff played that position with unparalleled fervor. He was a portrait of controlled violence and a man whose play was ruled by his extraordinary athletic ability and emotions. Sam may have been a nice guy off the field, but on the field he was anything but. He didn't like anyone who wore a different color jersey, and he believed that if he could hit you hard enough, not only would your helmet come off but so would your head!

At the time of his retirement, Huff's 30 interceptions was an NFL record for linebackers.

Players like Sam Huff proved that pro football will always be a hitter's game, a game of guts and guile played by men who deserve the respect and admiration of fans everywhere.

—Steve Sabol, president, NFL Films

FIRST QUARTER
A PATH WITHOUT BOUNDARIES

The Son of a Coal-miner

What do I want out of life? What do I want from myself? Am I going to spend the next 30 years working within a predetermined set of boundaries? Will I spend my free time on activities invented by someone other than me? Will I build my life around someone else's blueprints, only to look back and ask myself at 70 years of age, 'That was it?' I decided early in life that I would take a different path, one without boundaries.

I came into this world as Robert Lee Huff on October 4, 1934. The fourth of six kids, I was born in a mining camp in Edna Gas, West Virginia, but grew up just west of the Monongahela River Valley in another mining camp called Consolidation Coal Company Number 9, a few miles outside of Farmington, West Virginia. Thirty-four years later, on November 20, 1968, this same coal mine would claim the lives of 78 miners when high levels of methane gas and inadequate ventilation resulted in a catastrophic explosion.

To say that West Virginia coal mine life during the 1930s was tough is a brash understatement. The life of a coal miner parodied the words in the 1955 song "Sixteen Tons" sung by Tennessee Ernie Ford, "I owed my soul to the Company store." The coal companies owned their employees both body and soul; and some made the ultimate sacrifice.

The coal companies employed the miners to dig the coal under inhumane conditions, then turned around and rented them company houses and sold them their goods at the company store. The miners and their families gave their all just to stay alive, while the mine owners made a killing on the sweat and blood of their workers.

My family and I were no different from the other coal mining families. We lived on an old, dirt road in a small row house owned, of course, by the mine, which lacked even the smallest of luxuries, like running water. Since we didn't have a bathroom, there was a community pump outside for water and an outhouse located about 50 yards up the hill behind the house. Times were hard for everyone.

To get inside the house, you would walk up a flight of stairs into our living room. All that was there was a sofa, a chair, and our only source of heating, a potbelly coal stove. We had two bedrooms; one belonged to my parents and the other was shared by the six children. The entire time I was growing up, I slept in the same bed with my older brother, Don.

Back then, only the rich had rugs in their homes. I still remember how cold those row house linoleum floors were.

My father, Oral Huff, like his father before him, worked his entire life in the coal mines. From age 13 until his death in 1970 at age 63, it was the only life he knew. He suffered a series of heart attacks and was consumed by the insidious black lung, which had, in one way or another, affected every miner. I remember my dad coming home every night and coughing up black mucus. It didn't take me long to realize that this was not the life for me. As a matter of fact, it forced me to work that much harder at everything I did, just to be sure that I didn't end up emulating the life of my father.

Dad wasn't very big in stature. He was 5'7" at most and only weighed in at about 150 pounds, but he was one tough man, and strong as a bull. But his fate paralleled that of so many other coal miners. A series of heart attacks and the deterioration of lung tissue caused by black lung disease would, in the end, force my dad to succumb to his illness.

When he was working in the mines he ran what was called a loading machine, but I've been told he could work any job they gave him. There wasn't a piece of machinery that he couldn't fix and he truly loved working those mines.

I guess you could say that with the exception of each of us loving our chosen professions, we had very little in common. He enjoyed working deep in the depths of the mines; I was scared to death of them. He loved fishing and hunting as much as I loathed it. I developed a hatred for guns and killing at an early age.

When I was about three or four years old I had a pet dog that I really cared for. One day he somehow got loose and ended up being shot by the dog-catcher. To make matters worse, I saw the entire ordeal unfold right before my eyes. It was an extremely traumatic experience for a young boy to witness, and I truly believe that is why, to this day, I avoid guns and the sport of hunting.

My dad led an extremely tough life, but he always found a way to provide and keep the family together. By the time World War II got underway, the coal mines were operating 24 hours a day, seven days a week. It wasn't uncommon for Dad to work three eight-hour shifts back to back just to accumulate a little extra time to hunt or fish. Through it all, I never once heard him complain.

Payday was every two weeks, and like everyone else, we lived paycheck to paycheck. I remember once seeing my dad's paycheck after the company had deducted the rent and store money. It totaled $13.

The company owned our home. We bought our food, clothing, and necessities at the company store. I can remember how it was considered a big outing for my mom, Catherine, and my dad to travel 10 miles to Fairmont where they could grocery shop at a regular store.

As little as we had, I never felt poor. Everyone in the mining camp had exactly what we had. None of us knew any better. As a child, I only owned one pair of shoes, and they had to last all year. Mom had taps put on the heel and toe of each shoe so that they wouldn't wear out as fast. Then when spring came along, we'd kick free of our shoes and keep them off until the chill of October was upon us.

With Dad working at the mine all day, my mother was in charge of the house. That was no easy chore, either. Taking care of six kids while doing all the cooking and cleaning without the luxury of modern day appliances was not an easy task.

When Dad would arrive home in the evening from working all day at the mine, he would be completely covered with coal dust from head to toe. All that was visible were the whites of his eyes. I can still remember him coughing and spitting up all that coal dust lodged in his lungs.

As soon as he walked in the door, Mom would have him sit in a tub of hot water—the same tub she used to wash our clothes. As soon as he submerged his body in the tub, the water turned black. This became a daily ritual for him and was probably the only relaxation he experienced all day.

Dad had the opportunity to bathe on a daily basis, but us kids had to wait until Saturday.

Even though my dad was known for his easygoing personality, he was strict when it came to disciplining his children. He always carried a razor strap with him, and wouldn't hesitate to use it on us when we needed to be put in our place. The responsibility of the family garden fell upon my brother Don and me. With both of us more interested in playing sports than spading a garden, we tended to either do it at the last minute or, sometimes, not at all. But with a shoddy or unfinished task came horrific repercussions.

When my father would arrive home and see what we had done, or didn't do, out came the strap. Don and I both knew that we were in for it. My brother got it worse than I did, but I think that was because he was the older sibling. But let me tell you, when the strap came in contact with your skin, it really stung! My dad would hit you so hard that welts would immediately rise on the skin.

When our punishment had been completed, my brother and I would go over to our mother for comfort. She would always rub Vaseline on our bruises. Before I continue, I need to verify that this form of punishment was not done out of cruelty. That's just how things were done in those days. If you didn't do what your parents wanted you to do, you were punished. The same thing applied in school. If you didn't listen to your teacher or if you showed disrespect for authority, they had the right to whack you. It wasn't referred to as child abuse or neglect and no one considered it as such. It was just the way things were.

My mother was the one who was in charge of the finances and the one who kept everybody and everything together. With money as tight as it was, my mother had to make the most out of each and every dollar; and believe me, she did. She would buy everything she needed at the store, and what she didn't buy we would get from our garden.

I remember her bringing home a large beef bone or ham hock to make soup. After she added the vegetables from our garden, there would be enough soup to last a week. Our garden fed us year-round, as my mother would can many of the vegetables for use in winter. To this very day, her baked bread was the best I've ever tasted. Just thinking about it still makes my mouth water. Another of my favorites was the hamburger and fried potatoes she used to make. Since butter was too expensive back then, my mother would buy a pound of oleomargarine and add orange coloring to it to give it the look of butter. She would then place the margarine in a frying pan and cook the hamburger and potatoes in all that grease. It may not have been the healthiest choice of food, but it sure tasted great. I'm also sure that, along with all that coal dust, those diets were a contributing factor to the heart disease.

My brother Don was four years my senior and we were constantly at each other's throats. The fact that he was older than me made his life seem more attractive and, therefore, I wanted to hang around him and his friends. Of course, being the younger brother, Don would never allow it. We fought day and night, and let me tell you, those were some of the toughest battles I ever experienced—even tougher than confrontations that I dealt with on the gridiron.

Because he was older and bigger, he would beat the hell out of me, but I was never one to give up on an opponent. I would go so far as to throw objects at him, whatever I could get my hands on, whether it be rocks or sticks. One day he made me so angry that I grabbed one of Dad's pistols, put it up against his head and pulled the trigger. Thank God the gun misfired.

Don grew up to be a big man, 6'3" and over 250 pounds. Like me, my brother was a good athlete in high school, but unlike me, he never had the drive and passion to dedicate himself fully to any one sport. Like my dad, he enjoyed hunting and fishing, and at 16 he quit high school to go to work in the mines. In those days it was not uncommon for kids to drop out of school in order to go to work and help out the family financially.

One day my brother decided that he would take my dad on a hunting trip to Romney, West Virginia. For Don to get the time off, he had to work three straight shifts in the mine.

While the two of them were walking through the hunting grounds, my brother began to experience pain in both his chest and arms. All of a sudden Don collapsed right there in front of my dad. Having experienced a few heart attacks of his own, my dad immediately knew what had happened and went to get help. But by the time he had returned, my brother had passed away. He was only 35 years old.

My love of sports was always a driving force in my life. I always found time to play baseball and football in that small mining town. Due to the fact that we didn't have a great deal of sports equipment on hand, you had to be creative with what you did have. We made our own baseballs from an old sock that we stuffed with newspaper and straw. We would then wind thick, black electrical tape around the sock until it was hard and round in shape. Broomsticks emulated bats. We also made our own footballs.

Nobody had televisions then so our only link to the world outside was the radio. My favorite shows were Roy Rogers and Gene Autry. I would have given anything to have a pony, but of course, my parents could never afford such a luxury. My love for horses continues to this day, and I honestly feel that those old-time cowboy shows had a lot to do with it.

The Pittsburgh Pirates were my favorite baseball team, and Ralph Kiner was one of the early heroes of the era. But I couldn't wait for the West Virginia football games to be broadcast over the radio. I knew each and every player on that team.

One of my gridiron heroes was Frank Gatski. Like me, he grew up in the Number 9 coal mining camp. He was one of the fortunate ones who was able to go to college and play football for Marshall University. He was later a star lineman for the Cleveland Browns. Little did I know that someday Gatski and I would become teammates on a far more distinguished team: the Pro Football Hall of Fame.

A Mining Town Education

With the exception of college life, my entire educational career was centered within the mining town of Number 9. My elementary school had a population of 100. The school employed only a handful of teachers and a principal. That principal was Blair Wolfe, who was a strong believer in his faculty teaching the basics of education: reading, writing, and arithmetic.

The school was made up of three floors, and each floor housed two grades. The first and second grades were on the first floor, third and fourth on the second, and fifth and sixth on the third.

Mr. Wolfe was a strict disciplinarian, as were his teachers. I can still remember getting whacked on the knuckles with a ruler for not writing my letters correctly. Again, that's the way it was. If you didn't do it right, you got hit; and to make matters worse, your parents always sided with the teacher or principal.

I was the type of student who did minimum work, basically just enough to get by. With life already as tough as it was, education took a back seat to hard work in coal mine No. 9. It was rarely discussed among our parents, and the thought of attending college was more or less out of the question.

Like most boys my age, my favorite part of the day was recess. Mr. Wolfe would take us out to a pasture to play baseball or football, depending on which season it was. We couldn't play in the school yard because it was the mine's dumping site for waste materials. These slate fields surrounded the school like a moat. If you tried to play on them, you would rip your clothes to shreds, and none of us could afford to do that. Our wardrobe consisted of a couple of pairs of bib overalls, a T-shirt, and a heavy coat for the winter. I wore the same type of outfit until I entered high school. The first time I ever felt like a grown-up was in high school when I put on a pair of regular jeans with a belt.

Back in those days I had a best friend by the name of Leo Coceano. His family arrived in America from Italy when Leo was only four or five years old. When we first met, he couldn't speak a word of English. Our dads worked in the mine together, and Leo and I eventually became best friends, and were virtually inseparable.

We were not only best friends, we were also great rivals. The caliber of our athletic ability was fairly equal. Leo would have to be the captain of one team and I'd be the captain of the other. If we ended up playing on the same team, we'd always triumph.

I remember one time when Principal Wolfe was umpiring one of our games. I was pitching and was getting pretty hot over some of his calls. The final straw came when I threw a ball that was right over the plate and he called it a ball. I totally lost it. I called him a cheater and every other word I could think of. That didn't sit too well with him. He stopped the game, walked briskly and directly over to the pitcher's mound and picked me up by my shirt. He shook me so hard that he popped off every button. He also said that that was the last game he would ever umpire for us.

Organized sports did not come into play until high school. A few miles from Number 9 was Farmington High School—population 700 students. All boys who grew up in a mining camp were expected to play football. All girls were expected to become a cheerleader or play in the school band. In seventh grade, I met a girl by the name of Mary Fletcher, who played the French horn. We became boyfriend and girlfriend, and in our senior year of high school we were married.

I played football and baseball, and a little basketball until I was thrown off the team in 9th grade by coach John Victor for swearing. At the time, it really hurt, and I never again played organized basketball. To this day, Coach Victor revels in the fact that he can tell people that he was the only coach to ever kick a Hall of Fame member off his team.

From 1947 through 1952 I attended high school. Throughout those years I never once played against a black athlete in any sport. Blacks were not allowed to go to our school because of the segregation laws. Even though our fathers worked side by side in the mines, the black and white communities were separate. It wasn't that we didn't get along, it was just the way things were done back then. Desegregation laws did not come into effect until 1954, and when they did, the transition was smooth—at least it was in that part of the state.

Coach Kelly and Farmington High Football

I tried out for the high school football team my freshman year. I was 14 years old and ended up almost quitting after the first week.

Our coach was a man by the name of Ray Kelly, and he was an avid believer in fitness and conditioning. There were many times throughout the season when I honestly didn't think I would survive the workouts. He literally ran us until we dropped.

Coach Kelly was an alumnus of Farmington High and a veteran of World War II. In 1946 he returned to West Virginia to teach and coach. He was a wonderful man and the kind of person you could go to if you had a problem or needed to talk.

Upon making the cut, my first objective was to obtain a uniform. There were more players than there were uniforms. I had made what was called the second team, what is commonly known as the junior varsity. I played both offensive guard and tackle, and on defense I played lineman. I didn't play line-backer until I reached the pros.

Let me tell you, Coach Kelly held some tough practices. Once, after we had lost a game, some of the guys were jokingly saying, "Coach Kelly would probably keep us out at practice until the moon came out." Well, the bad news is that he heard us. He came out of his office and into the locker room to announce, "Boys, I wouldn't want to disappoint you. We will practice until the moon comes out." And needless to say, we did.

Back when I was in high school, the most common formation used in football was the single-wing, and everyone on the team played both ways. I personally never had the desire to carry the football. Besides, I didn't have great speed, didn't have running back speed. I was more of a contact person. I loved to hit, and I grew fond of the defensive line. My friend Leo played right next to me on defense at end. By the time we reached our senior year in high school, most teams made it a point to avoid running toward our side of the field.

Another desire of mine was to earn and wear a letterman jacket, the kind that said All-County on the back. I also wanted an All-State patch. Talk about being motivated! It was during this time that I decided to finish high school and go on to college to become a football coach, just like Coach Kelly.

Principal Joseph Cotrel

The students at Farmington High were a close-knit group. We all rode the bus to and from school. Since I had football practice after school, I usu-ally hitchhiked home. The principal of our school was a tough disciplinarian by the name of Joseph Cotrel. He began his career at Farmington in 1924 as a teacher, but by 1930 he had worked his way to the top administrative position. Back in those days we were disciplined with a paddle, and Principal Cotrel wouldn't even have given it a second thought if you stepped out of line.

I remember this one time when he paddled me good, and to make matters worse, I was totally innocent. What happened was, the boiler room was where the guys used to go to sneak a smoke. To this day I have never smoked. The idea of inhaling all those harmful substances never impressed me much.

Anyway, one day my buddy walked out of the boiler room with a cigarette in his hand. He was invited to shoot hoops with some of the guys and gave me his cigarette to hold. Just as he handed it to me, Mr. Cotrel turned the corner and caught me. Back in the day, you weren't given due process. You were guilty— no pleading, no nothing. He brought me to his office and really paddled me. What made it worse was that I really believe he enjoyed punishing big football players like myself.

A Routine Procedure That Proved Almost Fatal

I really wasn't that big back then. In my sophomore year I weighed about 150 pounds. But a strange thing happened the summer I had my tonsils removed. This occurred just prior to my junior year. I began to gain weight at a rapid pace. I really can't say that the tonsillectomy was a direct factor to weight gain, but by my senior year I tipped the scales at 210 pounds.

Having your tonsils removed as a child was routine, an extremely common practice back then. You spent a couple days in the hospital and then you went home. It was that simple. But in my case, I was lucky to even be alive.

Complete recovery from a tonsillectomy should take only a week or so, but by the following weekend, I was still sick in bed. That same weekend I developed a nosebleed. Having had them before, I laid my head back and waited for the bleeding to subside.

That same day the doctor who had performed the procedure had decided to go for a ride with his wife through the Farmington area. He stopped by to see how I was doing. Damn good thing that he did, because my nosebleed turned into a massive hemorrhage. My parents weren't at home and, time being of the essence, the doctor placed me in his car and rushed me back to the hospital.

At first the hospital refused to admit me without the consent and signature of my parents, but my doctor became so irate that the staff at Fairmont General Hospital allowed him to perform the procedure without the presence or consent of my mom and dad. Thank God they did, or otherwise I would have bled to death.

The End of My High School Career, Marrying Mary, and College Recruits

My junior year at Farmington High was one of its better football teams. Even though we were considered to be one of the smaller Class B schools in the state of West Virginia, we were pretty damn tough. One of the downfalls of playing for Farmington was its football field. It was located in a small valley and lacked the luxury of bleachers; therefore, we did a lot of traveling. If by chance we did play a game there, the fans had to sit on the banks of the hills to see the game. We played against Class A schools because they had a far larger enrollment than we did and our school would profit greatly from the gate receipts.

Back then we didn't have the comfort of a bus to take us to away games. We would caravan our players in crowded cars while our cheering fans followed behind. It was at this time that I met a man by the name of John Manchin, who owned a furniture business in Farmington. John would go on to play a major role in my life. He was so kind and considerate to both Mary and I. He bought me my first suit and my first car. John also gave me my first job, and when I went on to West Virginia University, he hired Mary to work for him. I helped out when I could by working weekends and vacations.

We played Fairmont High under the lights at a place called East-West Stadium. They often drew as many as 3,000 people per game! The roar of the crowd would at times become thunderous. I swear it was louder than anything I ever heard at Yankee Stadium, and that was even during the glory days of the Giants.

By the time I reached my junior year, I'd begun to gain confidence in myself. When we played Benwood Union High School, I remember one of their coaches yelling to his team from the sidelines, "Run the ball away from Huff!" That alone told me something about myself, something that no one else had ever said to me. I believed I could really play this game, and play it well.

The day before the last game of the season I attended a birthday party for a friend of mine. I had a hell of a time hitching a ride home and missed curfew by about five hours. Word got back to Coach Kelly and he benched me for the next game against our biggest rival, Monongah. Not only was I upset about not playing, but even some of the teachers were upset. One of our history teachers, J.W. Thomas, asked Coach Kelly to reconsider his punishment. Thomas reiterated the consequences to Kelly, "If you hold out Sam from the game, even the goal posts won't be safe." That still wasn't enough to make Coach to change his mind. And he stuck to it—well, sort of.

The ball was kicked off, and I just sat there on the bench. It was late in the first quarter, and Monongah had moved the ball up and down the field. Fortunately for us, they were unable to score. It was then that Coach Kelly walked up to me and said, "Well, Sam, I hope you've learned your lesson." With that, he put me in the game.

Benny Salopek was Monongah's star quarterback. I lined up and set my sights on him. As Benny dropped back to throw a jump pass, I completely unloaded on him. I hit him so hard that he was forced to come out of the game. A couple of plays later, his coach put him back in the game, but he was useless. He couldn't throw because of a shoulder injury that he'd incurred when I hit him. Salopek ended up having a broken shoulder, and we won the game 13–7.

The game was over and our team went back to the locker room to change. All of a sudden Jim Feltz, the Monongah coach, burst into our locker room and began ranting and raving at me for intentionally hurting his quarterback. He called me every name in the book and accused me of playing dirty. I hit Salopek with a clean, legitimate shot. There was nothing illegal or dirty about it.

Coach Kelly finally made his way over to Coach Feltz and escorted him out of the locker room. I'm surprised Kelly didn't haul off and hit him after the accusations he threw at me.

We finished the year with a 6–3 record, and I was named Second Team All-Conference. I was also beginning to gain some notoriety from the media and the colleges.

In my senior year, Harold Lahar, a football coach from West Virginia University, came out to scout one of our biggest games of the year against rival Riversville High School. He was interested in looking at Rudy Banick, a quick little halfback from our team, and a fullback by the name of Rob Toothman who played for Riversville.

At the end of the game, Coach Lahar approached Coach Kelly and said, "That kid Huff really impresses me. I'll be keeping my eye on him throughout the year."

Coach Kelly never said a word to me about his conversation with Lahar, but I soon found out that West Virginia wasn't the only school that was interested in me. By this time I weighed about 210 pounds. I felt that we had a good team, but our local newspaper, *The Fairmont*, didn't see things quite the same:

> Farmington High School lost 14 of their seniors to graduation this year. This loss will surely have an impact on the performance of this year's team. The players in general are medium-small except for the big and agile Sam Huff. The six-one husky stars for Farmington's sandlot baseball contenders (*I was a pretty decent catcher in those days*) and shows no awkwardness for his age and runs like a truck...an All-Conference choice in our book.

It turned out that the paper was right about me, but wrong about our team. We tied our first two games, but ended up winning seven straight and finished undefeated for the year. Against Romney High School I recovered a fumble and ran it in for a touchdown, the only score of the game. We won 6–0.

A complex point-scoring system that was used to determine who would play in the state championship kept us out of the running, but all in all, it was a memorable season, in more ways than one.

First and foremost, Mary and I married that year. We were both extremely young, but back then it was not out of the norm to do so. We had known each other since seventh grade, and dated throughout high school. I was so poor that when we were dating, I would wait for Mary to pay her way into the theater, buy popcorn, and sit down. Then I would pay my way in and share her popcorn with her. That was basically all I could afford.

As far as academics went, I was a better than average student, but never really applied myself to my studies. I was president of the Letterman's Club and even got a part in our school play, *We Shook the Family Tree*.

Farmington High's yearbook was named *The Lincolneer*, and I was described by my senior class as such:

> This good-looking boy is our muscle man
> At football he is great
> Sammy used his brains as well as brawn.
> He made first team, Class B, All-State

By now, I had been receiving letters from various colleges to play football. Army was very interested in me; that is, until they found out I was married. That was definitely against West Point's rules and regs. Florida also contacted me. They flew me out to the campus (my first ride on an airplane) and had one of their players pick me up. That player was star quarterback Haywood Sullivan. Haywood was supposed to show me around campus, but once he dropped me off at the college, I never saw him again. He went on to play professional baseball and once owned a piece of the Boston Red Sox. I always used to kid him about that weekend. I tell him that the money he was supposed to have spent on me during that visit probably went toward his purchase of the Red Sox.

It Would Be West Virginia

In the end, there was really no choice but to go to West Virginia. After all, Morgantown was only 30 miles down the road from me. Growing up I had listened to their football games on the radio. The voice of the Mountaineers was Jack Fleming. I knew all their players and followed them in the papers. When they recruited me, I was the happiest guy in the world. I was also the first in my family to ever attend college.

The coach of West Virginia was Art "Pappy" Lewis. He was a large man with great big bushy eyebrows and an incredible reputation for recruiting talent.

Joe Marconi, a fullback from Pennsylvania and my best friend at West Virginia, told me a funny story about Coach Lewis. He told me that Pappy wouldn't leave his house until he agreed to play for West Virginia. He stayed and ate with the family until the food ran out, then he would have a beer with Joe's dad.

Pappy always referred to his players as sons. He called his defense "hunters" and "walking dogs." When scouting running backs, he would say, "Does the boy like the briar patch?" That was his way of saying, "Can the player handle contact inside, or does he run to the water cooler?"

Back in the day, colleges were able to bring you to their campus in your senior year of high school. They had offered me a scholarship and I had already signed a letter of intent to play for them. One weekend in the spring, West Virginia invited me down to Morganville to visit their campus. They gave me a sweatsuit that had West Virginia written across the front of the sweatshirt. I was proud as hell to wear it. I don't think I took it off the entire weekend.

At tryouts, Coach Lewis and another coach, Gene Corum, wanted me to hit the blocking sled. Hell, I'd never even seen a blocking sled in high school. That's because we couldn't afford them. The only blocking and tackling I knew was against another player.

Coach Lewis weighed about 250 pounds, a big man for his time. He and Coach Corum stood on this big sled and told me to hit it. I thought to myself, "I'm gonna kill that sled, just break it in half and impress these guys." I threw myself into it all right, and the spring recoiled and shot me back 10 yards.

There I was, lying on my back on the ground with Coach Lewis standing over me. He turned to Corum in disgust and said, "Aw hell, Gene, there goes another wasted scholarship."

Pappy Lewis and the Mountaineers of West Virginia

Born February 18, 1911, in Pomeroy, Ohio, Art Lewis, like many of his players, was raised on a farm. He was a great tackle at Middleport High School, which was just across the Ohio River from West Virginia. Upon graduating high school, Art did what most of the boys did, he worked in the mines.

Two years later he traded in his hard hat for a football helmet and enrolled at Ohio State University. He acquired the name Pappy because he was the only 21-year-old freshman at the university.

Between 1932 and 1935 he played offensive tackle for Ohio, earning All-American honors in his senior year. He completed his collegiate career by appearing in the 1935 East-West Shrine Game. After graduating in 1936, Coach Lewis was drafted in the 1st round (9th overall) by the New York Giants, though his career in the pros was short lived.

After playing only one year for New York, Pappy left the game to become an assistant coach at Ohio Wesleyan University, only again, to leave a year later to join the Cleveland Rams as a player and assistant coach. Midseason, Pappy became the interim head coach. He was only 27 years old and at the time was the youngest head coach in NFL history. He finished the season with a 4–4 record and decided to stay on with the Rams as a player in 1939.

Like the majority of the young men of his time, Coach Lewis served in World War II. Upon being discharged at the end of the war, after three years in the navy, he became the head coach of Washington and Lee University. It was here that he found his niche in recruiting. Pappy left Washington and Lee to take the position as head line coach at Mississippi State University, but a year later—in 1950—Coach Lewis found himself a home when he was appointed head coach at West Virginia University.

By the time I had arrived at West Virginia in 1952, the team had gone from a 2–8 season in 1950 to a 5–5 season in 1951. Pappy was now establishing himself as one of the country's best college recruiters. In the past, many of the state's top football players would wind up playing for other colleges. Pappy changed all that, and by the summer of 1952, the West Virginia Mountaineer football team was primarily made up of the state's native sons.

Pappy's greatest season at West Virginia came in 1953. We went 8–1 in the regular season, losing only to South Carolina; captured the Southern Conference (SCC) title; and began a three-year winning streak against our rival Joe Paterno and his Penn State team. That same year the 10th-ranked Mountaineers played in the Sugar Bowl against an 8th-ranked Georgia Tech team, but lost by a final score of 42–19.

Under Coach Lewis West Virginia continued to dominate the SCC by winning the title four more times. In 1958 and 1959 the team began to decline, and at the end of the '59 season Pappy resigned to join the Pittsburgh Steelers as a scout. He remained with the Steelers until a heart attack claimed his life on June 13, 1962. He was only 51 years old. To this day he is considered one of the greatest coaches in West Virginia history and was inducted into the West Virginia Sports Hall of Fame in 1966.

The years that I played as a Mountaineer are referred to as West Virginia's "Golden Age" of football. Over the four years we played for Pappy Lewis our team proudly boasted a 31–7 record and produced six All-Americans: 1952, tackle Ben Dunkerley; 1953, guard Gene Lamone, center Bob Orders, and fullback Tommy Allman; and 1955, tackle Bruce Bosley and me.

I headed out for football training camp in the summer of '52. My wife, Mary, was living with her parents in Farmington and working for John Manchin. As a matter of fact, she stayed in Farmington throughout my college years. During my freshman year our son, Sam Jr., was born, which made it even more difficult for Mary to leave home.

When I arrived at camp, I didn't have a clue of what to expect. Our training facility was held at a beautiful 4-H camp in the north-central part of West Virginia known as Jackson's Mill. We had two-a-day practices and lived in the bunkhouses on the grounds. Complete solitude surrounded the facility and the chances of getting in trouble were slim to none. The field that we practiced on doubled as a landing strip, and to make matters even more difficult, we had to cross a creek on one of those old swing bridges just to get to it.

1952: A New Beginning

DATE	OPPONENT	SCORE
Sep 27	Furman	(L) 14–22
Oct 04	Waynesburg University	(W) 49–12
Oct 11	Penn State	(L) 21–35
Oct 18	Washington & Lee University	(W) 31–13

Oct 25	AT Pittsburgh	(W) 16–0
Nov 01	George Washington	(W) 24–0
Nov 08	AT Virginia Military Institute	(W) 39–21
Nov 15	Virginia Tech	(W) 27–7
Nov 22	AT South Carolina	(W) 13–6

1952 would be the year that West Virginia football began its reign in the SCC. Five freshmen formed a nucleus that would continue to have a major impact on Mountaineer football for the next four years. Each of us developed our own game, but the one thing we had in common was winning.

Pappy always had an eye for talent. Our quarterback, Freddy Wyant, was a cocky, left-handed passer from Weston, West Virginia, whose team had won only two games his entire senior year. But that didn't sway Pappy from recruiting Wyant as a Mountaineer. When he returned to campus, Pappy told one reporter that he had, "Just seen a boy who will make a great coach some day." As usual, Coach Lewis was right on the money.

Another recruit brought in by Pappy was a big, strong tackle from Greenbank who'd played fullback in high school. His name was Bruce Bosley. I remembered Bruce from basketball. In my senior year I went to Morgantown to see the state high school basketball tournament. One guy stood out among the rest. That guy was Bosley. At that time, he was the best built man I had ever seen, and he must have weighed 240 pounds. This guy was all muscle. He reminded me of the cartoon character L'il Abner. Opponents would try to get by him on the baseline, but all they did was bounce off his massive frame.

Pappy also added two great running backs that year. Bobby Moss was an All-State recruit from Huntington and Joe Marconi was a 220-pound fullback from Fredericktown, Pennsylvania—approximately 30 miles from Morgantown. Marconi and I became best friends, took all of our classes together, and roomed together for the majority of our four years at West Virginia.

That year, Marconi didn't show up at camp right away because he had decided to attend the University of Maryland. Coach Jim Tatum told Joe that he would be the only fullback recruited that year, but when Marconi showed up at UM training camp, they were already seven deep in the fullback position.

Joe immediately called Pappy and showed up in time to start the season for West Virginia.

What I remember most about that first year was training camp. Like Coach Kelly, Coach Lewis was adamant about conditioning. We'd be on that practice field for an eternity. He used to bring in teams like the Quantico Marines to scrimmage us. It was literally a game of boys vs. men, but we held our own.

We opened up our season against Furman. We thought we could beat them, no problem, but our arrogance got the best of us. Me made a ton of mistakes during that game and ended up losing 22–14. Late in that game, though, Coach Lewis decided to give Freddy Wyant a chance. After all, what the hell.

Freddy came in the game and threw a long TD pass, but it was too little, too late. The positive side to it all was that Coach now had himself a quarterback for the next four years. We had a great offense with Wyant running the split-T with a fullback and two backs. We were a running team with a great deal of option plays and a group of guys who could overpower their opponents—well, most of them.

Early in the season we lost to Penn State 35–21. The Lions had a big, tough tight end by the name of Jesse Arnelle who no one could stop, not even me. This was our second loss of the season. It was also our last. We went on to win our final six games and finished the year with a 7–2 record. That was the last time we lost to Penn State during the four years that I played for West Virginia.

Throughout the '52 season, the collegiate rules allowed for what was called two-platoon football. Two-platoon football designated eight players, each who played only on offense or defense. I spent most of the season playing middle guard on defense and part of the season playing tackle on offense. In 1954, the NCAA emplaced a set of new rules requiring the use of the one-platoon system. This system allowed only one player to be substituted between plays, which effectively put an end to the use of separate specialized units.

My first year as a Mountaineer was devoted totally to football. I lived in the men's dormitory (the school didn't have co-ed back then) and I despised it. Each room was shared by two guys, and each bathroom was shared between three or four dorm rooms. Coach Lewis felt that the athletes should mingle with the rest of the school population, so I was given a non-athlete as a room-mate. It would have been much easier to bear if the athletes had all roomed together.

Here's one example why: One night, somewhere around four o'clock in the morning, a guy from the dorm room next to mine came into my room and pissed all over my foot. He had been out partying all night and was totally inebriated. He thought my room was the bathroom. I quickly set him straight and sobered him right up on his directional skills. Hell, I went ballistic and almost killed the bastard! He's damn lucky to even be alive.

Another thing that didn't sit well with me were the fraternities. I remember those idiots walking around campus during pledge week with their little beanies on their head and carrying those stupid paddles. I thought they were all crazy, and I personally didn't have time for that kind of bullshit.

Getting back to Pappy, he was adamant that his players attended *all* of their classes. Marconi and I very seldom missed a class. At that time I was a physical education major and was planning to teach and coach football. Pappy had a monologue that he used to preach to the team, "Now, boys, I can do a lot for you if you play for me here at West Virginia. But if you don't attend class, I can't help you, and personally, I don't want you around."

If you did something wrong during a game or at practice he would say, "If you don't like it, you can go get yourself a good ol' number three shovel and go back to the mines."

That was all I needed to hear. Working the mines was a fate worse than death.

We Had The Entire Town Behind Us

In today's game you see a montage of prima donnas and spoiled athletes. These guys are usually the same players who were paid off while in college. In fact, as the joke has it, some of these college kids took a pay cut when they entered the pros.

Back in '53 no one considered himself better than the next guy. Football was not the sometimes 'individual' sport that it is today. We played as a team and everyone gave 100 percent of his skills, talent, passion, and drive. Sure, some of the townspeople like Freddie Cavallaro, who owned a bar in Morgantown, would do things for us like feed us chili and cheeseburgers while we were playing pinball at his establishment. We didn't have a lot of money and the merchants would help us out from time to time.

Another guy by the name of Harry Goldsmith owned a clothing store. If you were fortunate enough to be named Player of the Week by the Mountaineer coaching staff, you could go to Harry's shop and pick out a new tie, belt, or shirt. He would even put your picture in the store window for all to see.

If you went to a movie, the usher at the door would let you in for free. The same went for Chico's Dairy Bar, where you would be served a soft drink for nothing if you didn't have the money for one. It was all very innocent.

Because I was on an athletic scholarship, my room, board, and tuition were paid for, and I received approximately $10 a month to do my laundry.

The atmosphere in the college locker rooms was a far cry from what you see today on collegiate campuses. The fat-cat alumni weren't seen hanging around our locker room after each game like they do today. As a matter of fact, I didn't even hang around there after the games. The only time I could go home and see Mary was on the weekends, so after each game, I would get dressed, hitch a ride to Manchins' grocery store, and help Mary close up for the day. One minute I was a football hero, and the next I was stocking shelves or sweeping the floor while my wife tallied up the day's receipts.

My social life on campus was virtually nonexistent. My daily routine never changed. I attended classes and went to practice. On the weekends, I went home. During the week we would sometimes play intramural basketball or softball. The football players would always get a basketball team together. With Bosley and me playing forward, no one ever tried to come up the middle for a layup. If they did, they got flattened.

At the end of my freshman season I returned to Farmington, where Mary and I rented an apartment above a small grocery store. Our place was located about a block away from where Mary's parents lived. It was far more comfortable and relaxed not living with her relatives. We'd finally gained some privacy in our lives. Besides, her father and I never saw eye to eye. He never did like me much, and the feeling was mutual. Like my dad, he'd been a miner, and like others who worked the mines, he ended up retiring on a disability. On the positive side, being a block away from her parents allowed for us to have full-time day care for Sam Jr. while Mary was at work and I was back at school.

Throughout my four years at West Virginia, I continued to work for John Manchin. While Mary worked at his grocery store, I worked for his furniture company. You name it, I did it. I sold, moved, carried, and delivered. I was paid minimum wage and occasionally, when the economy tightened up, I never saw a paycheck, but John was always there for the both of us when we needed him. I'd like to think he thought the same about me.

Back in 1968 a horrible fire gutted John's furniture store. He lost everything. At that time, I wasn't making a great deal of money, but I still managed to send him a check for $10,000. I honestly couldn't afford it, but it didn't matter. I knew John would pay me back. That was the kind of relationship we always had. As a matter of fact, my final three years of college weren't spent in the dorm but rather in a trailer in Morgantown that John owned. I shared it with three other football players. This allowed us all to save a couple of bucks. Space was tight and the four of us shared two double beds, but you do what you have to do to get by.

The Entrepreneurs

Joe Marconi and I were nicknamed the Gold Dust Twins because we were always trying to make a couple of bucks on the side.

During basketball season, Joe and I cut a business deal with the building superintendent. We worked for a dollar an hour doing menial jobs such as cleaning and sweeping up after games. We also supervised the parking lots. Joe worked one lot and I worked the other. We'd charge two dollars per car for parking. The media parked free, but everyone else had to pay. Plus, we got to keep the money. We also got to know the state trooper who watched the door and cut a deal with him. He charged people five dollars to stand and watch the game. One particular night when our big Mountaineer basketball star, Hot

Rod Hundley was playing, Joe and I ended up splitting $300 all in one-dollar bills. That was the total take from the parking lot and the standing-room-only crowd.

When I arrived home that night, I showed Mary the money and threw it on the bed. The first thing she said to me was,

"Where did you get all that money?"

"Robbed a bank," I told her.

She immediately began to cry. She'd actually believed me.

One night while working the parking lot, the wife of our basketball coach drove up to the lot. I didn't recognize who she was, and of course asked her for two dollars.

She was pissed.

"I'm the coach's wife and you're going to charge me two dollars to park?"

Nervously, I replied, "No, ma'am. You just park wherever you like."

The athletic director soon got wind of the incident and not only did we lose our parking lot jobs, we were also fired from our maintenance jobs. Anyway, it was nice while it lasted, and what the hell, we were just two poor jocks trying to make a buck.

Tommy Allman, Doc Morris, and The Nutcracker

Because we spent the majority of our time with our teammates, it was no wonder that all our friends were football players. That suited me just fine.

One of my best friends was a fullback by the name of Tommy Allman. The way he pounded guys back then would now be considered borderline inhumane. After graduating college, Tommy ended up selling insurance. I'm sure many of those guys wished they'd had a policy back then.

One guy in particular, Jesse Arnelle, should have been a policy holder. It was during my sophomore year that Tommy hit Jesse so damn hard that he broke his nose. Arnelle was never the same after Tommy got through with him.

Tommy hailed from Charleston, West Virginia, and loved to fight. Even though he never lifted a weight in his life, I truly believe that he could have taken on any of today's players. That's how tough he was. He was always in trouble with the coach because he screwed around at practice, but when it came time to play on Saturday, he gave 110 percent. I guess that's why Pappy loved him the way he did.

We were never allowed to practice on our home field. The university wanted the grass perfect for game day, so we ended up taking a bus to another field located on a separate part of the campus. That field was pretty chopped up. One day, Tommy thought he would warm up barefooted. While practicing though, he stepped on a piece of glass and completely tore up his foot. This was three days before we were to play Pittsburgh—one of our biggest rivals.

Tommy received stitches in his foot, but was still able to start the Pitt game on Saturday. After a few plays, I noticed that he was in pain. He finally came out of the game and hobbled over to old Doc Morris who was standing near the team bench. Doc had graduated from Maryland in *1912*.

"Hey Doc, my foot is killing me. You gotta' give me something for the pain," Tommy said.

When Doc Morris pulled off Tommy's shoe, his sock was soaked in blood.

"Well, son, I've got to pump a little painkiller into that foot."

He took a syringe out of his medical bag. I swear, the needle looked like it was a foot long. It made me queasy. Tommy placed his foot on the bench and without even removing the bloody sock, Doc jammed the needed right through his foot. And this was done in front of the entire fan base. They didn't even bother to take him to the locker room. Tommy just put his shoe back on and finished the game. Talk about tough. But that was Tommy Allman, tough as hell.

For some reason the athletes and the equipment managers never got along. They constantly gave the players a hard time. One specific day, our equipment manager, Soupy Roberts, got into it with Tommy. Here's what happened.

Soupy gave Tommy an old pair of shoes to use for practice. Tommy didn't like the way they fit, so he asked Soupy for a new pair. Of course, Soupy refused his request. He told Tommy, "You can't have a new pair because we don't have any for you right now."

Apparently Tommy didn't buy his story, and instead he took a big cardboard box and went around to each player's locker. Inside that box he put every pair of shoes he could find, carried the box past the coaches' offices and out the door. There was a river near the campus and Tommy threw all those shoes over the side of the bridge into the water. With that, we all got a new pair of shoes.

The irony of it all is that Tommy didn't even get in trouble for what he'd done. I truly believe that some of the coaches were afraid of him. He was then and still is the toughest guy I have ever known.

There was one incident, though, in which Tommy got me in big trouble with Coach Lewis. It happened during my sophomore year. The Mountaineers had been playing poorly and Pappy was extremely dissatisfied with our performances. He was so upset that he decided that he would bench me. I felt that the punishment was more to psyche me up, but that didn't keep me from getting pissed off.

After conveying to the team his frustration with them, we all hit the field for practice. We knew we were in for it. Anyway, there I was, pouting because of being benched and, because of that, dogging the run.

Tommy knew I was mad. He saw me running half-speed and yelled out, "Hey, Sam, how come you're not running?"

I yelled back to Tommy, "When you play second team, you don't need to work out hard, you don't need to run."

I wanted Pappy to hear me, and he did, and he was steaming mad. He ran over to me, grabbed me by my jersey and said, "Let me tell you something, Huff. You'll run when I say run, and you'll shut up when I say shut up. Now when I put you down, you had better run!"

All I could say was, "Yes sir!" Then I ran like hell.

One of the things I really liked about Coach Lewis is that he would always tell his players, "If you think you're better than the guy playing ahead of you, come and tell me and I will arrange to see who should be playing."

That's exactly what I did.

Coach Lewis loved competition and told me, "Okay, we'll do the nutcracker drill tonight at practice."

Before I continue, I need to explain what the nutcracker drill is.

First, you took two blocking bags and placed them side by side, approximately three yards apart. Next, the two players competing against each other faced off in that three-yard space and went head to head. The player who was still standing at the end of the competition took over the starting position.

That night, Pappy matched me up against a senior by the name of Frank Federovitch, who was the starter for that position. There'd already been bad blood between us, as he was one of those frat guys. I outweighed him by 20 pounds and just dominated him from the get-go. Coach Lewis stood by his word and I took over the starting position for the next game.

1953: The Greatest Team in Mountaineer History

DATE	OPPONENT	SCORE
Sep 26	AT Pittsburgh	(W) 17–7
Oct 03	Waynesburg University	(W) 47–19
Oct 10	Washington & Lee University	(W) 40–14
Oct 16	AT George Washington	(W) 27–6
Oct 24	Virginia Military Institute	(W) 52–20
Oct 31	AT Penn State	(W) 20–19
Nov 07	Virginia Tech	(W) 12–7
Nov 14	South Carolina	(L) 14–20
Nov 21	AT North Carolina State	(W) 61–0
Jan 01, '54	Georgia Tech	(L) 19–42

West Virginia's 1953 football season is usually considered the greatest team in Mountaineer history. Our first five games were victories, including a 17–7 domination of Pitt, who held the mighty Oklahoma Sooners to a 7–7 tie a week later. I was the starter at both the defensive and offensive guard positions. Two weeks later we crushed Washington and Lee University 40–14, which gave the Mountaineers their 300th win of the West Virginia football program. After annihilating the Virginia Military Institute 52–20, the college bowl scouts began focusing on the Mountaineers.

28

Following our 20–19 victory over Penn State, the Sugar Bowl committee began to show a great deal of interest in us. It was during that game that Bosley blocked a punt and recovered it in the end zone for the winning score. The Nittany Lions had fielded a great team that year. One of their stand-outs was a 290-pound tackle named Roosevelt Grier. We ended up playing on the Giants together and becoming good friends, but throughout our college days there was definitely no love lost between us.

Grier was also the first black player I'd ever played against. Of course, playing against him had nothing to do with what color he was; my only concern was finishing the game in one piece.

The line coach at West Virginia was Russ Crane. Every spring he would work with Bosley and me on specific blocking and tackling techniques to stop Rosey. Russ had figured out the best way to block Grier was to hit him low. It proved to be an effective weapon against him. Another trick he showed Bruce and me was how to grab a player and not get called for holding, but that's another story.

That same year, Pappy told me that if I could outplay Grier that he'd get me a suit of clothes. After beating Penn State and controlling Grier, I called him on it, and he was true to his word. There was only one problem though, Pappy never said he would get me a *new* suit of clothes, just a suit of clothes. So he gave me one of his old suits. It was a size 52, three sizes too big, with huge lapels. I swear, it looked like something out of a mafia movie.

Anyway, in week seven we saw Tommy Allman run for 55 yards in the fourth quarter to help us beat Virginia Tech 12–7. It was also our 7th straight win of the season. The following week we weren't as lucky. In front of a record 31,000 fans in the stadium, South Carolina beat us at home on a fourth quarter punt return. Final score: West Virginia 14, South Carolina 20.

The following week we not only demolished, but shut out North Carolina State 61–0 at Raleigh. The Sugar Bowl came calling and on January 1, 1954, West Virginia was matched up against Georgia Tech, their legendary head coach Bobby Dodd, and their versatile quarterback/placekicker Pepper Rodgers. Rodgers would go on become Tech's head football coach from 1974–1979.

This bowl game should have been one of the major highlights of my collegiate career, but instead, it turned out to be one of the most humiliating and depressing experiences I've ever had.

The bowl committee treated this event as though it were a holiday. That was their first mistake. Next, they flew the wives down with the team. That was their second mistake. Third, we reported to Biloxi, Mississippi, two weeks prior to the game. Tech arrived the weekend of the game. This should have been treated as just another road trip, but it wasn't.

Biloxi was located approximately 70 miles from New Orleans, where the game was to be played. Pappy was a little concerned, as were many of us, about being so far away from home. Many of the players had never left the hills of West Virginia. Here's what Pappy had to say at a New Orleans quarterback club luncheon, "Some of these boys have never been out of the hills and you can't tell what will happen when they get to this part of the country. But no matter what happens, they'll be hitting hard on New Year's Day."

That's right. You can't tell what will happen, but I knew right away that it was wrong to bring the wives. Mary became homesick after only a short time. She was unhappy because she wanted to go on all the New Orleans tours and see the shows. We couldn't afford to pay for those kinds of luxuries, but she went anyway. I stayed in the room and just steamed.

A couple of nights before the big game a team banquet was held on our behalf. Just as the banquet began, Pappy got up and said, "Boys, I want you to look under your plates right now."

We all looked under our plates, and I'll be damned if there wasn't a brand new $20 bill waiting there for each of us. As for me, personally, it was the first 20 I ever had that was all mine.

It was also the first time that I'd eaten shrimp. Sure, I had used shrimp for bait, but eat it? When they served us shrimp cocktail at the banquet, I said, "Are you crazy? There's no way I'll eat that fish bait!"

Well, one of the players talked me into trying it with mustard sauce, and I'll be damned if it wasn't really good. It's too bad I can't say the same for the way we played against Georgia Tech.

Tech was a great passing team, and defensively we were not good with passing teams. Our defense had been designed to stop the run, and with Rogers quarterbacking, they killed us. The stats proved it. Rogers was 16–26 for 195 yards with three touchdowns. Final score: Georgia Tech 42, West Virginia 19.

To this day, that game leaves a bad taste in my mouth. The officiating was horrendous. One of the bad calls occurred when Tommy Allman took a pitch out, ran to the outside, and sprinted 60 yards for a first-quarter touchdown. Just as Tommy broke free, the official looked at me and threw his handkerchief.

"You're holding!" he said.

"Hell, I never even touched the guy!" I yelled back.

While reviewing the game films, I noticed that no one on the line had held. I truly believe that because we were a Northern team playing a Southern team in the South, the officials were biased toward Tech. There is no doubt in my mind that the officials were responsible for the final outcome of that game.

1954: An 8–1 Season and No Bowl Offer

DATE	OPPONENT	SCORE
Oct 02	AT South Carolina	(W) 26–6
Oct 09	George Washington	(W) 13–7
Oct 16	AT Penn State	(W) 19–14
Oct 23	Virginia Military Institute	(W) 40–6
Oct 30	Pittsburgh	(L) 10–13
Nov 06	Fordham	(W) 39–9
Nov 13	AT William & Mary	(W) 20–6
Nov 20	North Carolina State	(W) 28–3
Nov 27	AT Virginia	(W) 14–10

With our only loss to Pitt, the 1954 Mountaineer season was a total success. Not only did we win eight games out of nine, we beat Penn State for the second year in a row. But I think that because of the poor showing we had in

New Orleans, the major bowl committees were uncertain about granting us another bid, regardless of our 8–1 season record.

I know we would have handled a second game differently because of our past experience, but that didn't change the fact that we weren't invited that year. After that horrific loss against Georgia Tech at the Sugar Bowl in '53, the Mountaineers would not be invited to another bowl game until 1964, where they would lose to Utah State 32–6 in the Liberty Bowl.

The last time West Virginia was invited to a bowl game and won was in 1948 when they played Texas Western in the Sun Bowl. They wouldn't win another bowl game until 1969 at the Peach Bowl, where they would defeat South Carolina 14–3.

On November 13, while we were playing William & Mary in Williamsburg, Pennsylvania, an explosion took place at the Jamison Mine No. 9. If the explosion had taken place one hour earlier, I would have been the only surviving male member in my family. That day 15 miners lost their lives.

1955: Penn State Loses a Record 3 Years Straight!

DATE	OPPONENT	SCORE
Sep 24	Richmond	(W) 33–12
Oct 01	Wake Forest	(W) 46–0
Oct 08	Virginia Military Institute	(W) 47–12
Oct 15	William & Mary	(W) 39–13
Oct 22	Penn State	(W) 21–7
Oct 29	AT Marquette	(W) 39–0
Nov 04	AT George Washington	(W) 13–7
Nov 12	AT Pittsburgh	(L) 7–26
Nov 19	Syracuse	(L) 13–20
Nov 25	AT North Carolina State	(W) 27–7

We came out of the chute with a seven-game winning streak. Our fifth game of the season was against Penn State—a team we had beaten both in 1953 and 1954.

The 1955 campaign found us projected for a top-10 finish by the polls. We finished the season with an 8–2 record. It was also the third year in a row that we won the SCC, but once again there was no bowl bid.

That same year the Mountaineers recruited a guard/center by the name of Chuck Howley, who later would be drafted by the Chicago Bears and end up as a star linebacker for the Dallas Cowboys. Chuck was a hell of an athlete and was a great asset to the team.

That 1955 season saw West Virginia beat Penn State for a third consecutive time. I know our team not only impressed then head coach Rip Engle, but also his young assistant coach, a guy by the name of Joe Paterno.

Years ago, while I was a radio broadcaster for an Alabama-Penn State game in the Sugar Bowl, I had the opportunity to introduce myself to Joe Paterno. This is how incredible the man's mind is.

I said, "Coach, I'd like to say hello. I'm Sam Huff."

He looked at me and said, "No. 75."

"No, sir. I wore No. 70."

"Not at West Virginia you didn't," he said. "You know, Sam, we had another assistant who did the scouting for us and when he gave the team his report, he'd always give everybody's number. I'll never forget this scout telling us that everybody talks about the left tackle, No. 77, Bruce Bosley, but that Huff, No. 75, he's the guy who's killing everybody. Nobody talks about him, but he's the guy you better watch out for."

Coach Paterno really made my day.

My senior year also saw me get knocked out for the first time. We were playing Marquette in Milwaukee when all of a sudden my lights went out. When I came to I was on the sidelines and no one could tell me what had happened. It wasn't until we watched the game film the following week that it became clear what had happened to me.

The player who had been playing opposite me hauled off and cold-cocked me in the jaw with his fist. He just flattened me, and to this day I have no memory of that game. I also found out that he had been Marquette's heavyweight boxing champion. I could understand why.

The Best Damned Football Player You've Ever Seen!

In his sophomore year at Syracuse, Jim Brown was the second leading rusher on the team. As a junior, he rushed for 666 yards, and by his senior year he was a unanimous first-team All-American. He finished fifth in the Heisman Trophy voting and set school records for highest rush average and most rushing touchdowns.

That was the man I was going up against.

Just prior to the game, one of our scouts, Russ Crane, came into a meeting and said to us, "Gentlemen, I want to tell you something. Syracuse has a guy who's the best damned football player you've ever seen. His name is Jim Brown, he's 6'2" and weighs 232 pounds. He wears No. 44—and he has he ability to go all the way every time he touches the ball. You better keep it away from him. Don't even kick it to him."

I took that spiel as an insult. We may have been a little cocky, but hell, we had just as good of a team as they did. Besides, we never paid all that much attention to the opposition. In this case, though, it proved to be a costly mistake.

November 19th finally rolled around and there we were at the start of the game. I really wasn't worried, and besides, we had home-field advantage.

We were in our huddle before the opening kickoff. Back in those days, I had a pretty good leg and handled the kickoffs. Just then Wyant came up to me and said, "Don't kick it down there. Jim Brown is down there."

As I looked down the field, my eyes focused on the biggest running back I'd ever seen. He had the perfect football physique: huge shoulders and arms, small hips, and huge legs. I have to admit, he was a bit intimidating, but what the hell. I knew I wasn't going to kick it to him because the wind was blowing in my face from the open end of the field. I told Wyant, "Don't worry about Brown. I can't kick the ball that far."

Or so I thought. I ended up kicking the ball right to him. As he made his way up the field, he ran over us as though we weren't even there. Once he got into open field, he changed gears and wasn't caught until Bobby Moss tackled him on the 10-yard line. It was now first and 10 and Joe Marconi was playing the linebacker position. Brown not only came through the hole, but ran right over Joe and scored. The six points were called back on a penalty, but it didn't matter. A few plays later, they scored again. Brown had made a lasting impression on us.

We were leading 13–7 at the half, but just before the third quarter was about to begin, Brown came over to me and said, "The first half was yours, baby, but this one's ours."

It was early in the third quarter of the game when Jimmy barreled through a hole in the line and I was there to greet him. The head-butt that I planted on him was so hard that my headgear snapped down and broke my nose. The pain from the break was so devastating that I immediately reacted by clamping my teeth together. The force of the bite was so powerful that it sheered the enamel right off. Did I mention that I was knocked-out cold?

When I awoke in the training room I was still a little lightheaded. On my head rested an ice pack and there was blood oozing from my nose. The pain radiating from my teeth was unbearable. Even though my nose had been broken and I had suffered a concussion, it was my teeth that I was most concerned about. I had always had a nice smile and now it was ruined. As I lay there running my tongue over the rough surface of what was left of my pearly whites, I began to shout, "My teeth are gone! My teeth are gone!"

I will never forget my introduction to Jim Brown. He may have won the first battle, but over the next 10 years, I eventually won the war.

SECOND QUARTER
START SPREADING THE NEWS—THE NEW YORK GIANTS

Hot Tempered, Arrogant, and Out of Control

Welcome to the NFL! We might draft you first, but you come into camp dead last. Your stats don't matter. Your awards don't matter. So you better bring heart. Bring all the pride, talent and determination you've got. Prove yourself to the veterans and they'll be the first to pick you up. Show this staff you can finish and they'll call your number. Help take this team to the next level and the fans will not only scream your name, they'll wear it!

That was the attitude of the NFL—the National Football League—but for some guys, that acronym came to mean Not For Long. I almost became one of *those guys*. Here's how it all began.

A few weeks following the conclusion of the collegiate football season, the NFL commenced with the first part of its player draft. Back in '56 the NFL was highly concerned about the competition from the Canadian Football League, so the first three rounds of the draft were held in December. They wanted the best collegiate players under contract as soon as possible. You have to remember, this was long before the glamour and glitz of today's draft. There wasn't any big buildup in the media or predictions of who will go where in what round. Personally, I didn't really know that much about the NFL draft or even pro football for that matter. Actually, I really wasn't that interested in the idea of playing professional football.

As a kid, I used to listen to the Pittsburgh Steelers games on the radio, and I knew that the Cleveland Browns had a player from my hometown of Farmington by the name of Frank Gatski. But it ended there. I just figured that my career in football would be over following my senior year. After completing my degree I would find a job teaching and/or coaching.

Another component of the draft was that they lacked in sophistication. Scouts were few and most teams drafted from the All-American lists. Bruce Bosley and I had been chosen for most of the All-American teams. The years I made it, he didn't, and vice versa. I was once told that the reason we both weren't consensus All-Americans is that the sportswriters were not comfortable with selecting two players from the same team at the same position. Whatever the reason, it didn't take away from the fact that Bosely was a great football player. I loved the game and was happy just to be out on the field. I later found out that it was *because* of Bruce that the Giants were interested in me.

The Giants had sent a scout by the name of Al DeRogatis out to West Virginia to take a look at Bosley. Back in the early '50s DeRogatis was a starting lineman for New York. Knee injuries forced him out of the game, but like many other former NFL players, Al went on to become a great football analyst for the networks.

Upon his retirement from pro football, the Giants hired him to scout the colleges. In the fall of '55, he wrote the following in his report:

Bosley is great, but there's another guard down there who will be even greater. His name is Sam Huff.

Based on that report, so I'm told, is how the New York Giants made me their third-round draft choice—30th pick overall in the NFL's 1956 Draft. Bosley was drafted in the second round, 15th overall by the San Francisco 49ers, and Joe Marconi went in the first round, 6th overall to the Los Angeles Rams.

Neither Bosley nor Marconi nor I knew what to make of the draft. Hell, the Giants didn't even ask me to come to New York after I had been chosen. I read about it in the newspaper.

New York didn't contact me until a few weeks later. I had been selected to the *Look Magazine* All-American Team and was flown out to New York for a photo shoot. I was pretty impressed. *Look* picked up the tab for everything, including sending a plane all over the country to pick up each of the All-Americans.

When we arrived in New York, we were greeted by our hostess, an up-and-coming actress by the name of Kim Novak. There was this cocky, 20-year-old junior halfback from Notre Dame who immediately began making moves on her. His name was Paul Hornung and he was a first-team All-American.

He was also a first-team skirt chaser. Novak came across as standoffish and distant, and Hornung never did score.

I have to admit, though, we had a great time in the Big Apple, and there were some great players on that All-American team: Howard "Hopalong" Cassady, a great running back from Ohio State and the 1955 Heisman Trophy winner; Earl Morrall, the crew-cut quarterback from Michigan State who beat UCLA in the '56 Rose Bowl; Jim Parker, a massive guard from Ohio State who was known for his strength, size, and quickness, and helped Woody Hayes and his Buckeye team to win their first national championship in 1954; and Rommie Loudd, an end from UCLA who was drafted by the San Francisco 49ers but instead signed with the BC Lions of the Canadian Football League. In 1960 he signed with the newly formed AFL and joined the Los Angeles Chargers.

We spent a week in New York. A big dinner was given in our honor at Gene Leone's Restaurant. We were all given a Lord Elgin watch and later appeared on the *Jackie Gleason Show*. While I was staying at the Hotel Lexington in Manhattan, Wellington Mara, the then owner of the Giants, called to meet with me. He wanted to discuss my contract. Hell, what did I know about contracts? But I agreed to meet with him. In those days you didn't have agents or attorneys to negotiate for you. If you had, the owners wouldn't even talk to you and you would have been blackballed from the league. Playing out your option and free agency hadn't been invented yet.

There was what was known as a "gentlemen's agreement" among the owners which meant that no team would sign another team's players. If you didn't like what was being offered in your contract, you could always hold out. But unlike today, that very seldom worked out.

Mara met me at the Hotel Lexington and we discussed my contract with the Giants. Wellington offered me $5,000 for the year to play in New York. I may have been a country boy from West Virginia, but I told him that I couldn't support my wife and child on $5,000 a year. He asked me what I would play for, and I told him $7,000. He told me that he might be able to work that out. Before I signed anything, I told him that I had to run it by Pappy Lewis. So I called Pappy.

"Mr. Mara wants me to sign for $7,000. What do you think?"

"Son," he said, "that's like stealing money. You get right back over there and sign that contract before he changes his mind."

Without hesitation I immediately signed my first pro contract. Wellington then asked me if I needed any money. I told him that Mary and I had just purchased some new furniture and were in debt in the amount of $500.

"No problem," he said and wrote me a check for $500.

I thought that the check was a bonus. But when I received my paycheck after the first game of the 1956 season, I immediately saw that $500 had been deducted from my pay. I went and asked Wellington what was going on. Why was I shorted $500?

"That's the advance I gave you when you signed the contract. You gotta learn, Sammy, that in this business there's a big difference between a bonus and an advance."

I never did get that $500 returned, but it taught me an important lesson about pro football and the people who held the power of the game in their hands. It may look like just a game, but in reality it's a business—big business—and don't ever forget it.

That was the last time I would be contacted by the Giants until the following summer. It was then that I received their letter telling me when and where to report to training camp. That was it. The system that is used today is completely different. A freshman college prospect gains immediate attention from the pros the day he walks on campus. The scouts attend your practices and combines. They weigh you, time you, analyze your skill, personality, temperament, and drive while at the same time watching hours upon hours of film. Once you are drafted, you are given a playbook to memorize and you are evaluated for a conditioning program. You attend minicamps for rookies and find that there is basically no off-season. You learn their system long before you go to training camp in July.

Following my final season of collegiate football, I played in the North-South game in Florida as well as the Senior Bowl in Mobile. I very seldom missed a class—the very thought of not graduating on time never even occurred to me. Hell, I was going to be the first person in my family to obtain a college degree, and I wasn't about to screw that up.

In the spring I played baseball. I was catcher for our West Virginia team and did well enough to capture the attention of the pro scouts. In fact, I was signed by the Cleveland Indians' Class A minor league team in Reading, Pennsylvania. My contract was extremely meager, but I figured I could play pro baseball until the pro football season started in August.

It wasn't long until I realized that pro baseball was a waste of my time. My main job that summer was to warm up the pitchers in the bullpen. The minor league manager was a guy by the name of Don Heffner, and he never even put me in a game to see what I could do. Finally I went up to him and asked why I wasn't playing. He told me he wanted to see how I did up against a good pitcher. The following day at batting practice I consistently knocked the ball out of the ballpark. I saw Heffner walking toward me, and I figured he was going to tell me what a great hitter I was.

"We think you can hit," he said, "but we don't think you can catch good enough to make it in the majors."

I told him I was outta there. Besides, I wasn't that crazy about baseball life. The bus rides were long and dreary, and you were forced to stay in these fleabag YMCAs. The food was less than edible and you waited all day just to play a night game. What was worse is that I wasn't playing. I was just along for the ride. To this day I don't know why the Indians wasted their time on me. I was just glad to get out of the game when I did.

In early August both Bruce and I drove to Evanston, Illinois, to practice for the College All-Star Game. The game was played for the *Chicago Tribune* charities, and we practiced at Northwestern University. It was a place for sports reporters to hang out along with the hundreds of fans who came to watch us practice. Our coach that year was Curly Lambeau, founder, player, and first coach of the Green Bay Packers. He was a well-groomed, well-dressed guy who always smoked a cigarette in a holder. He looked more like he belonged on Park Avenue than on a football field. As I think about it, he really didn't do much coaching. We just ran some basic plays. I played offensive guard and never even practiced with the defense. I didn't mind. There was just one goal

I had in mind, to be introduced with the starting lineup, and I was. That has always been a strong motivation for me, to be noticed and recognized, to be somebody.

Well, I received that recognition that I desired, though it came mostly from the referees. My opponent was the Cleveland Browns' veteran lineman, Don Colo. He immediately introduced me to submarine warfare. I got penalized three times for a total of 45 yards for throwing punches. I totally lost my temper. Colo kept head slapping me, which was legal then, and my ears continued ringing all through the night. I also received a valuable lesson that game: it's always the second guy in a fight who gets caught. Colo may have thrown the first punch, but it was my retaliation that the refs saw. The one thing I had to learn about professional football was that it was a form of controlled violence. It may be a violent game, but if you don't keep your emotions in check, you'll get thrown out every time, and that's a fact.

Cleveland had beat us—no, let me rephrase that—they *slaughtered* us by a score of 26–0. It was boys against men. You can't expect a group of recent college grads to go up against seasoned pros, especially a team that won the world championship earlier that year.

The following day, five All-Stars: Jim Katcavage, Don Chandler, Henry Moore, Hank Burnine, and I flew east to St. Michael's College in Winooski, Vermont, to join the New York Giants training camp. The Maras liked being associated with a Catholic school. In fact, when we broke camp, we trained at Fordham University. Wellington enjoyed being in the company of priests, and what the hell, it couldn't hurt.

When we arrived at training camp we were all still sore and stiff from the All-Star game. We had no idea of what to expect, and then we were told that we were all to take part in the team's regular scrimmage on Sunday. The vets had reported two weeks prior and we were now being thrown to the lions.

We met our coach, Jim Lee Howell, at our first dinner. He was from Arkansas and set in his ways. I disliked him immediately. He made sure that we knew that there was only one boss and the rules and regulations applied to everyone. There would be curfews and fines. Basically, he tried to put the fear of God in us, but it didn't work. In that spiel he talked about the scrimmage that was to take place on Sunday. He told us that the team that won would get the following day off.

Sunday morning we dragged our asses to the scrimmage and I played nose guard. It was almost like playing middle linebacker because you can hit and pursue and go anywhere on the field. I made a lot of plays that day, but there was one in particular that happened late in the scrimmage. Chandler went back to punt and I juked the center and nailed him. He fumbled and I picked up the ball and ran 60 yards for a touchdown. My team won the scrimmage and I couldn't wait to have the next day off. But it didn't work out that way.

Howell made us practice anyway. That didn't sit right with me. I've always believed that what a coach says ought to be law. I don't like people who lie to me, and I didn't like Jim Lee Howell.

In my opinion, Howell hated rookies. I would be out there busting my ass and he'd yell from across the field in that damn Arkansas drawl, "Huff, you're not running!"

Howell would push you to your limit and beyond, which is okay, but you have to know when to stop. Lombardi was like that. He was the Giants' offensive coach that year and he knew when to let a man breathe. Howell never knew how to do that. He never knew how to build a player back up.

I can remember times when I was so angry with that bastard that I wanted to literally kill him. I would hold on to my helmet and create visions of smashing it over his head if he said one more thing to me. To this day, I don't know why I didn't.

I ran into him years later, after the Giants had traded me to the Redskins. I told him how close he came to dying. I also emphasized how much I hated him and asked him why he had been such an asshole to the rookies. In response he just shook his head and said he didn't even realize he'd given that impression.

The veterans weren't exactly our best friends either. At that time there were only 33 players on the roster, and they all knew that the rookies were there to try and take their jobs.

During one of my first days of practice I saw an elderly, gray-haired man wearing a baseball cap, walking onto the field. I'd done some place-kicking in college, and I thought it would be to my advantage if I practiced some place kicks while I had the time. I yelled over to the coach, "Hey, Coach, where's the kicking balls?"

The man stopped in his tracks, turned around and just glared at me. It turned out that he wasn't a coach at all, but the Giants' veteran starting quarterback, Charlie Conerly. Boy, did I screw up and ol' Charlie was far from amused.

"Don't you ever call me a coach, you smart-ass rookie!"

And he wasn't joking either. Years later, we laughed about it, but when it happened, no one was laughing.

To make matters worse, I was homesick and hurting. I was continually being yelled at by Howell and no one even knew if I would be playing offense or defense, much less which position I would play.

We were now ready to play our first exhibition game against the Baltimore Colts in Boston. Most of the week during practice I played the offensive line and like other rookies, special teams. Baltimore had a running back called the Bronze Bullet. His name was Buddy Young. He was only about 5'4", but his quickness and acceleration were beyond anything I'd seen before. At the University of Illinois he was the NCAA champion in the 100 meters and tied the world record in the 60-yard dash. That's fast! Anyway, I was told that Buddy was extremely dangerous on punt returns.

I wasn't really worried about it because I still remembered what Ray Kelly had taught me at Farmington High School, "Sam, when you are running downfield on punts, always follow the ball."

I later found out that's exactly what you don't do, but I hadn't yet learned that. So we kick off and I follow the flight of the ball, never even bothering to look at how the blocking was forming right in front of me. Buddy caught the ball, took a couple of steps, and then cut around to go to the other side of the field. Just as he reversed his field I got blindsided and my knee buckled beneath me. I was in a world of hurt.

I had never had a knee injury before, and I couldn't believe how painful it was. I was sitting on the bench when it was time for the special teams unit to go out on the field. Walt Yowarsky, one of the Giants' linemen, saw that I was sitting there with an ice pack on my knee and said, "Hey, rookie, you're supposed to be out there. Now we [the veterans] gotta do it all!"

If I could have stood up, I would have punched him!

Transportation back to Winooski was by train and those guys wouldn't even let me have the lower berth. Bad knee and all, I was forced to climb to the upper berth. That's how much those guys cared about rookies. The sympathy didn't stop there, it carried on to the practice field. It didn't matter that you were hurt, you still had to show up for practice. I was forced to stand around those damn two-a-day practices holding 235 pounds up on crutches!

My morale couldn't get any lower at this point, and my roommate, Chandler, felt the same way as I did. I remember there was a popular song out at that time titled "Detroit City." One day it was playing on the radio and one of the lyrics really hit home. Every time we heard the words, *I wanna go home*, Chandler and I would tell each other that if we heard those words one more time, we were going home.

Sure enough, that damned song came on the radio. "That's it," I said. "Let's go!" And Chandler was right behind me.

I knew that we had to turn in our playbooks. Since I was still working out with the offense, I looked for Howell, but he was nowhere to be found. We saw Lombardi lying on his bed taking a nap between practices. We had the nerve to go into his room and wake him up.

"Hey, Coach, we wanna turn in our playbooks."

That was the first time that I had ever seen Lombardi get mad. He shot out of the bed and just ripped into us. He didn't hesitate to call us every name in the book either. Chandler took off like a shot, but I was stuck there unable to run because of my crutches. Lombardi finished ripping me a new one and then finally calmed down. I left his office still determined to go home.

As I was packing there was a knock on the door. It was our line coach, Ed Kolman. "They tell me you're homesick and want to leave, Sam. Is that right?"

"Yes, sir," I said. "I can't take another day of Jim Lee Howell's yelling and picking on me."

"Sam, you can be a star in this game. You can be a great player, but you've got to stay in camp and stick it out. If you stay, I'll talk to Jim Lee and get him off your back. But I want you to stay."

"For you, Coach, I'll stay."

There was just one problem: Chandler still wanted to go. He knew that Lombardi wouldn't take pity on a homesick rookie. Chandler talked me into going to the airport with him knowing that I had decided to stay with the team. I think he just wanted some company.

When we arrived at the airport we were forced to sit in the waiting room because there were no planes arriving or departing. All of a sudden we saw Lombardi barge into the waiting room. He snagged the team station wagon and raced all the way to the airport to talk Chandler and me out of leaving. He was very convincing. We both decided to give it another try.

Lombardi really liked Chandler and even traded for him when he left the Giants to become head coach for the Packers.

From that day on, Jim Lee Howell left us both alone, but he lost a lot of good players because of his unsavory attitude. I'm just thankful that I stuck it out.

From Tweener to Middle Linebacker

In the beginning I had the feeling that assistant coach Tom Landry didn't take a liking to me. It wasn't anything personal, it was just that Landry had more important things to do than to spend time with a rookie without a position.

I became what was known as a tweener. At 235 pounds I was too small to play offensive line and too big for linebacker. In training camp I continued to play both offensive and defensive line until late in the summer when I was assigned full time to Landry.

This was Tom's first year as a full-time assistant coach. He had just completed a great career as a defensive back for the Giants and for the past several seasons he'd been a player/coach after Howell had been named head coach in '54. Landry was now totally in charge of the defense. We had a regular middle linebacker by the name of Ray Beck who was an All-American at Georgia Tech. Tom had just begun to develop what is now known as the 4–3 defense with Beck in mind. Ray was an intelligent player and a real student of the game. That's exactly what Landry was looking for.

Due to the knee injury that I'd incurred while playing the Colts, I was forced to sit out most of the preseason games that summer. Back in the '50s the owners agreed to play six exhibition games. And why not? All the money that was made from those six games went to the owners. Many of our games were played in cities that didn't have an NFL team. The expense per player was only $10 a week prior to the opening of the regular season. We didn't have the benefits that today's player has, like health, disability, or life insurance; nor did we have any rights. If you didn't like the hand you were dealt you had two options: play it out or go home. That was it. Let me give you an example.

We had an offensive tackle by the name of Dick Yelvington. He was one tough guy. This one year we were out in Berkeley, California, for one of our exhibition games and the club set us up in this really nice hotel. In those days, many of the establishments didn't have free TV in the rooms, so some of the guys would go out and rent TVs. They figured the organization would pick up the tab. Well, they were wrong. The TV rental charge was a dollar a day, and when we picked up our paychecks the following week, those who rented TVs had the money deducted from their checks. Yelvington was visibly upset about it all.

As he got on the bus that same day to go to practice, he noticed Wellington Mara sitting there. He said, "I had a cup of coffee in the coffee shop, Wellington. Why didn't you take that out of my paycheck, too?"

Wellington didn't say a word, but Yelvington was traded soon after the incident.

Team essentials were also denied. While in camp, the equipment managers separated our practice uniforms in boxes. The jerseys would go in one box, the sweats in another, and the jocks in still another. I arrived one day to practice a little late. As I stood in line to get my gear, Wellington Mara was standing behind me. It was his daily ritual to change into sweats and cleats when he joined us on the practice field.

49

I picked out a pair of old sweatpants—the second-to-last pair left—and immediately found that the crotch was completely worn out. I figured that Mara would take pity on me and offer a new pair to practice in. After all, you wouldn't expect the owner of the team to wear these god-forsaken rags. Was I ever wrong.

"Hey, Sam, that's all we've got to work with. Just put a pair of shorts on underneath. They'll be okay."

Our locker room, too, left much to be desired. It was situated under the chow hall at St. Michael's. Each player was given his own space, which amounted to roughly the dimensions of a furnace room. There was no air conditioning in the locker room; therefore, on hot summer days it was about 20 degrees hotter than it was outside. There were far fewer showers than there were players and by the time you got dressed and walked outside, you would be completely soaked in sweat. Can you imagine what would happen in today's game if the owners tried to pull that? Most would likely strike. These spoiled prima donnas today have no concept of what the players of yesteryear had to deal with.

Anyway, getting back to Landry and the conclusion of the exhibition season.

My injured knee was coming along, but Ray Beck had a bad ankle. Our next game was against the Chicago Cardinals in Memphis, Tennessee, and Landry asked me if I had ever thought about playing the middle linebacker position. Even though my response to him was no, he still asked that I give it a try.

While at West Virginia, I played middle guard, what is now referred to as a nose tackle. I was used to playing in the middle of the defense. While Landry was experimenting with his 4-3 defense, and also working on the 5-2. I had been practicing at the nose guard position most of the summer, so when I made the move to middle linebacker it seemed to be the perfect fit for me.

My new position led to a great game against the Cardinals. I never missed a tackle. A great middle linebacker must possess the ability to tackle from anywhere at any angle. I had that ability and was a great fit for Landry's new design.

I felt pretty confident after the exhibition against Chicago, but Landry was not as confident and chose to start Beck in the regular season opener against San Francisco. With Beck's ankle improved, Tom chose to go with the vet, but it would be short lived. Ray reinjured his ankle and I got in for a few plays. My play wasn't as impressive as it was against the Cardinals, but I did contribute to a big win over the 49ers and their Million Dollar Backfield, which included quarterback great Y.A. Tittle.

Our second game of the season once again pitted us against the Chicago Cardinals, but this time it would be played on their home turf. 1956 was our first season at Yankee Stadium. The Maras had moved the Giants from our former home field, the ancient and dilapidated Polo Grounds, to a more modern facility at Yankee Stadium. Also, unlike the Polo Grounds, it had more than 67,000 seats. We were forced to open on the road because the New York Yankees' baseball season had not yet ended.

Even though Beck was on the injured list, Landry was still uncomfortable with starting me at middle linebacker. Instead, he moved Harland Svare from tailback to middle linebacker, but Harland could never take control of the position, and the Chicago game proved to be no different. The Cardinals also decided to throw a bombshell at us by coming out in a split-T offense centered on their great running back, Ollie Matson. Matson was 6'2", 220 pounds, and considered a really big back for the time. Not only was he big but he was fast as hell. To give you an idea of how fast he was, Ollie had won both a silver and a bronze medal in track at the 1952 Olympic Games in Helsiniki.

The second weapon was the use of an electronic device. Ray Richards, the Cardinals' coach, had been using transistors to communicate with his quarterback and his defensive captain to call all the signals. It's no wonder the Cardinals beat us 35–27.

As for me, it was an extremely frustrating day because the only time I saw any action was playing on special teams.

Our next game was against the Browns. Their coach, Paul Brown, also believed in the transistor system. He was using transistors to communicate back and forth with their quarterback George Ratterman. Even though our own coach, Jim Lee, did not believe in the use of electronic devices, we found a way to listen in on their wavelength. One of our rookies, an end named Bobby Topp, sat on the end of our bench and listened to Brown call the plays. Bobby would pass the information on to Landry, and Tom, in turn, would let us know which play the offense was going to run.

Unfortunately for us, the capacity crowd for the Cleveland home opener was too loud for Ratterman. He couldn't hear Brown calling the plays, so the electronic communications were quickly abandoned.

Once again Beck started the game but was forced to retire early in the game due to his injury. I finally got the call from Landry to replace Beck. As soon as Paul Brown saw that there was a rookie middle linebacker on the field, he made sure the play was aimed at me.

Cleveland liked to hand off the ball to Ed Modzelewski, a huge back and brother of my teammate, Dick Modzelewski. He was nicknamed Big Mo and every time we lined up in the 4-3 defense, Big Mo was coming right at me. Play after play I met him head-on while we found our way to Ratterman, sacking him six times. We ended up winning the game 21–9.

In my opinion, I felt that this was the best game I ever played. From that day on I became the starting middle linebacker for the Giants, and Tom Landry began to pay quite a bit of attention to me.

The Genius of Tom Landry

Like many of the players and coaches, I resided at the old Excelsior Hotel located on 81st Street off Central Park on the west side of Manhattan. Landry also lived there and each night he would come down to my apartment or I would go up to his to discuss defensive strategies. Actually that's how we developed the 4-3 defense.

We had the inside 4-3 where the defensive tackle would shut off the middle and the linebackers would pursue to the outside, or we'd go to the outside 4-3 where the tackle would angle outside and I would come up the middle and make a play in there, or catch the play from behind. All the years we played, that's all I ever did. We got so good at it that it became almost second nature to everyone in the unit. That first year, Landry called the signals. If he had his hand on his hip, we'd go to the inside 4-3. If he put his hand on his stomach, we'd throw in a blitz.

At first, he wanted me to play off the center and then pursue, but that caused me to get caught up in traffic, and wouldn't allow me to make the tackle. I came up with an idea, and asked Landry if we could try it out.

"Why don't you let Mo and Rosey Grier take care of the middle and let me go with the flow of the backfield?"

Tom liked the idea and put them both in a four-point stance. Neither one of them was happy about the move, but it worked. They were able to plug up the middle, which allowed me to move from sideline to sideline.

Landry was one of the first coaches to set up his defense against the strength of the offensive formation. Every offense and every defense have their strengths and their weaknesses. Tom would precisely set up the Giants' defense to play against the strength of their opponents' offense. We always lined up in a 4-3; therefore, the offense continually observed the same formation. But once the ball was snapped, everything changed, all depending on where we keyed our moves.

In the old days, a team would line up in a 4-3 and focus solely on the ball. The genius of Landry changed that. He told us to watch the way the backs lined up and to watch which side of the field the tight end and the flanker were lined up. Those became the keys to what the offense would do once the ball was snapped. We'd then roll our zone defense to the strength of the formation and react accordingly when the ball was snapped. The concept was actually very simple, and when we watched it on film it became a thing of beauty.

I always said that Tom Landry made me the first designated hitter in sports. His modus operandi was precision and discipline. He always treated his players as professionals. In other words, he expected them to play to the best of their ability, believed that's what they were getting paid for. You never saw him acknowledge a player with a pat on the back or tell a player what a great job he did, but you knew that he respected you, and you respected him.

Those who didn't know or understand Tom saw him as an unemotional person, one who didn't care about other people. Even some of his own players felt that he was cold, impersonal, and detached. Running back Duane Thomas referred to Landry as "that plastic man." That's because he and the others who felt that way didn't know him. If they had, they would know how very deeply he cared about his players. Once I asked Tom about his demeanor, and this is how he responded to me:

> "Sam, I believe my team reacts the way I react, so if I give in and get upset when one of my players gets hurt or goes down and I become too emotional, I think the other players would see that and maybe lose concentration on what they're supposed to be doing. I never want emotion to break my concentration on the task at hand."

Acquisitions and Veteran Talent of 1956

Not only did we have some pretty good assistant coaches, but we also had a very talented team. In addition to Chandler and me, the Giants had drafted a 6'3", 237-pound defensive end out of Dayton by the name of Jim Katcavage. We also picked up Andy Robustelli in a trade from the Los Angeles Rams.

Andy had made All-Pro with the Rams but was not happy with the way he had been treated by them. It all started when he had asked for permission to report to camp a few weeks late because his wife was ready to deliver their baby. Los Angeles gave him a hard time, so Andy threatened to sit out the season. Wellington Mara found out about this and called Andy personally to ask him if he would like to play for New York. With Andy living in Stamford Connecticut, he was more than happy to leave the West Coast and begin a new career with the Giants. Mara also knew that it would help with the fan draw. All in all, it worked out great for both player and owner. Mara received an All-Pro and future Hall of Famer and Andy went on to become the general manager of the team. How's that for a win-win situation?

A trade was also made with the Steelers to get Dick Modzelewski, the younger brother of Ed "Big Mo" Modzelewski of the Browns. Dick became a starter at defensive tackle. He was positioned next to Rosey Grier. Katcavage and Yowarsky covered the other side. The two linebackers were Svare and

Bill Svoboda. Svoboda became a Giant in 1954 and was one of the toughest men I ever played with. He only weighed 215 pounds but no one on the team wanted any part of him. At practice, Bill would hit you with everything he had, whether we practiced in pads or not. No one—and I mean no one—from the offense would be allowed to run around his end of the field. He hit everyone: Frank Gifford, Alex Webster, Kyle Rote, he didn't care who you were. Stars and backups got it the same. Svoboda played without a face mask. During a game his face would be a bloody mess. He looked like a nightmare coming at the opposing team.

Our defensive backfield was pumped up with players like Ed Hughes from the Rams, veterans Jimmy Patton, Dick Nolan, and a future Hall of Famer by the name of Emlen Tunnell. Thanks to Landry and his players, the defense finally received the recognition it so well deserved.

Lombardi's offense was equally as good. With Charlie Conerly at quarterback, Gifford and Webster at the halfback position, and Rote playing end we had a winning team in the making.

Even though Howell held the title of head coach, he knew he didn't have the expertise, knowledge, and coaching talent that Lombardi and Landry had. He used to tell the media that his job was to keep the chalk sharpened and the footballs blown up. Ironically, other than being the disciplinarian of the team, those were basically his only duties. He knew enough to let the masterminds of the organization run the team.

After practice many of the players would head out to the local bars like Toots Shor's or P.J. Clarke's. Toots loved the athletes and treated them like celebrities. He was also an extremely generous person. In 1956 he happened to acquire a stack of tickets for Game 5 of the World Series, and decided to give each player two tickets. I don't remember why, but I never did go to the game. Of course, that was the game in which Yankee pitcher Don Larsen threw a perfect game against the Brooklyn Dodgers, the only perfect game ever in the history of the World Series.

That was the extent of our life outside of football. Television had yet to surface from the backwaters of the American sports scene and into the mainstream. We could basically go anywhere and no one would recognize us, because they essentially didn't know what we looked like. Products would not be endorsed by athletes until the 1960s. That first year I didn't even own a car. My form of transportation was either by taxi or subway.

One day during my rookie season, I had to get to Yankee Stadium for practice so I decided to grab the subway. It was my first time on underground transit. I happened to get on with Dick Modzelewski. I figured he probably knew his way around New York being that he'd been in the NFL since '53. Boy, was I wrong. It was Dick's first time on the subway as well. Neither one of us knew that the subway we were on didn't even stop at Yankee Stadium. We ended up in upper Manhattan—in Washington Heights—and had to pay $20 for a cab ride back to the Stadium.

That Championship Season

We opened the '56 season winning two out of three away games. The first was a 38–21 win against the 49ers in San Francisco. Then we lost in Chicago against the Cardinals 35–27 and we followed that with a 21–9 win in Cleveland against the Browns.

For the majority of the 1956 season, Howell utilized two quarterbacks. The first quarter usually belonged to Don Heinrich. From the second quarter till the end of the fourth quarter, Charlie Conerly would take over. There was no rhyme or reason to the change, and neither Heinrich nor I could figure it out.

You wouldn't call Charlie a pure passer, but he always had a great feel for the game. His style was controlled, precise, and methodical. He was a quiet man, but there was no doubt that he was the team leader. I personally saw him as a grump. He would go for weeks at a time without saying as much as hello. I thought he was a tough old bird, but the reality of it was that he was only 36 years old at the time.

Charlie came across to others as unfriendly. He just wasn't a socially out-going kind of a guy. But on the field he was in complete control.

Conerly attended and played college football at the University of Mississippi. He originally started at Mississippi in 1942, but left to serve as a Marine in the South Pacific during World War II, where he fought in the

Battle of Guam. He returned to Mississippi in 1946 and led the team to their first Southeastern Conference Championship in 1947.

Charlie was acquired by the Giants in 1948, and by 1953 had considered retiring after being battered throughout a horrific 3–9 season. His offensive line was extremely inexperienced and Charlie ended up paying for it. In 1954 Jim Lee Howell took over the coaching duties for Steve Owen. He promised Charlie that he would improve his offensive line if Conerly would consider coming back. And, as they say, the rest is history.

We opened at home on October 21, 1956, to a crowd of 50,000. When I stepped into Yankee Stadium I was in awe of the historic arena. Just two weeks prior, Don Larsen threw the first perfect game in World Series history, and along with teammates Whitey Ford, Mickey Mantle, and Yogi Berra, had sat in front of the very same lockers that I and the rest of my teammates were now sitting. What an incredible feeling to be standing in the most famous stadium in America.

I'm sure we were all a little nervous, but we hid it pretty well. In front of the largest opening-day crowd in New York Giants' history, we ran over the Steelers 38–10. Gifford carried the ball seven times for 100 yards, and Conerly threw for three touchdowns.

Next we defeated the Eagles at home 20–3 and the following week played the Steelers in Pittsburgh, beating them this time by only a three-point differential. Final score: Giants 17, Pittsburgh 14. With a 5–1 record, we were ready to take on the Cardinals. This time, the game would be played in New York, and it would prove to be no contest.

With over 62,000 screaming fans at Yankee Stadium, Landry set me up to key in on the Cardinals' big back, Ollie Matson, and we held him to only 43 yards rushing on 13 carries. We crushed Chicago 23–10 and were now 6–1, having played our way to sole possession of first place in the NFL's Eastern Conference.

November 18 we played the Redskins in Washington and fell to defeat. Final score: Washington 33, New York 7. The following week we were back home, only to tie with the Chicago Bears, 17-all. In that game, Bears' receiver Harlon Hill made one of the greatest receptions that I've ever seen.

In the closing minutes of the game Hill managed to break free of double coverage when quarterback Ed Brown heaved a 56-yard pass downfield. Harlon tipped the ball at the 5-yard line, tipped it again at the 3, then dove into the end zone and caught the ball for the touchdown, tying the game.

The Redskins were our next opponents and with their 5–3 record, they were right behind us. This was a must-win game for the Giants. At least we had the home-field advantage. As it turned out, our defense played well, and Gifford had an outstanding day. He rushed for two touchdowns, caught a 14-yard pass from Conerly for another TD, and threw a 29-yard pass to Ken MacAfee for yet another score. Final: Giants 28, Redskins 14.

We didn't fare as well the following week against the Browns. They literally ran all over us. Between their quarterback Tommy O'Connell and their kicker Lou Groza, we didn't stand a chance. Frank scored our one touchdown, and we lost, 24–7. We were now 7–3–1 for the year. The Redskins were 6–4, and we had a must-win game against the Eagles in Philly if we wanted to capture the Eastern Division title.

That must-win situation turned out to be a cake walk. For the first time that I can remember, Heinrich played the entire game. Kyle Rote, Alex Webster, and Gifford all scored touchdowns. Rote's TD was on a six-yard pass from Gifford. The Eagles scored seven points in the fourth quarter but it was too little too late. Final score: New York 21, Philadelphia 7. Next stop, the championship game against the Chicago Bears.

It had been a long season and to tell you the truth, I was still in a daze the majority of that year. Hell, I was only 22 years old, still green, and only a year out of college. It's not that I didn't take the game seriously, because I did. It's just that I was young and overwhelmed by it all: the enthusiasm of the fans, the passion of the media, and the breathtaking ambiance of New York City.

I may not remember much about that time, but I sure do remember how cold it was. The week leading up to the championship game New York felt as cold as the North Pole. The field at Yankee Stadium had been covered with a tarp, but the cold was too much for it, and it froze solid. Back in 1934 when the Giants had won their first championship—also against the Bears—the team had played in basketball sneakers.

Our teammate Andy Robustelli had heard about this story through Wellington Mara. Andy owned a sporting goods store in Cos Cob, Connecticut, and a few days before the game he was informed about a new line of Keds that suctioned well on gymnasium floors. Robustelli got the go-ahead from Wellington and ordered shoes for the entire team. When we arrived at the stadium and saw the arctic field conditions, a few of the players decided to try out the shoes on the frozen tundra. They were amazed at how well they were able to maneuver on the icy turf.

We came out onto the field with the sneakers; the Bears came with their cleats.

Lombardi kept the game plan simple. So simple that the majority of the quarterback handoffs were to our big fullback Mel Triplett. Not only did he run right through the Bears' defense, but so did everyone else.

In the first quarter Gene Filipski blasted the Bears with a 53-yard kickoff return to the Chicago 38-yard line. Two plays later, Triplett went off left tackle, flattened umpire Mike Wilson, then carried three Bear defenders across the goal line for a 17-yard touchdown. Ben Agajanian, our kicker, scored two back-to-back field goals for six points, then in the second quarter, Alex Webster scored from three yards out for a 20–0 Giants lead.

I almost felt sorry for Bears quarterback Ed Brown. Almost. He couldn't do anything right. Our defensive unit just annihilated him along with their fullback Rick Casares. Casares was a tough runner and ball carrier, but I had my sights on him all afternoon and held him to only 43 yards rushing. Brown was held to a total of 97 yards passing all day.

The only time we were a little worried was when Emlen Tunnell fumbled a punt and Casares followed with a touchdown run, but that's where the Bears' scoring efforts ended. Following that unfortunate end to the shutout, we drove 72 yards, ending the drive with Alex Webster's one-yard TD. We sealed the coffin when Ray Beck blocked a punt and another Giant rookie, defensive back Henry Moore, fell on it in the end zone for a touchdown. The halftime score was 34–7.

At the beginning of the second half, the Bears made a quarterback change. George Halas sent in George Blanda to replace Ed Brown. We knew that

Blanda was the kind of quarterback to just stand back and throw. It made it simple for us to defend and a hell of a lot more fun.

In the third quarter Conerly threw a nine-yard pass to Kyle Rote for another six points, and in the fourth quarter Gifford snagged a 14-yard pass from Charlie to finish off the Bears. Final score: Giants 47, Bears 7. It was New York's first NFL championship since 1938.

I was awarded the distinction of becoming the first rookie middle linebacker to ever start on a world championship team, and was also named the NFL's Rookie of the Year. Gifford was named the NFL Player of the Year, and Rosey Grier was named the NFL's Lineman of the Year.

At the time, I didn't realize the significance of such an honor. I had never known defeat, as neither my high school team nor my college team had ever lost a championship game. It just didn't seem to be that big of a deal, at least not the way the Super Bowl is portrayed in today's NFL.

Of course, the winnings were a little different back in 1956 than they are today. In 2010 each winning player received a $83,000 bonus and a ring. Each losing player received a $42,000 bonus. Our payday for winning the NFL championship was $3,779.19. What I am about to tell you next would never, ever happen in today's insane world of the NFL.

Back in the day, the team voted on how the playoff money would be distributed. In other words, you had to vote to pay guys who had come and gone or had gotten hurt during the season. You also decided which coaches would get how much. If the head coach didn't like the way you voted, he would let you know. I can still remember Jim Lee Howell yelling at us, "I don't like that vote, now get the hell back in there and vote again!" Can you imagine telling the players of today that they had to vote to see who would get paid and how much?

One week prior to the championship game a historic landmark took place in favor of the NFL players. In November the players, through a collaborative effort, created the NFL Players Association. After meeting with the Commissioner and the owners, the NFLPA managed to secure some long-sought guarantees for the players. Among them, players would receive a minimum of $5,000 a year in salary, as well as uniform per diem pay. Clubs were now required to pay for players' equipment and, perhaps most important, a provision was created that mandated that an injured player continue to receive his salary.

1957: Wellington and Contract Negotiations

In this day and age when a team wins the Super Bowl, the players and coaching staff celebrate the victory all year long. It is a non-stop parade of personal appearances, commercial endorsements, and much, much more. When the Giants won Super Bowl XLII in 2008 against the New England Patriots, several books were published profiling the team, the stars, the coaches, and the season.

Following our 1956 NFL Championship there was some media coverage of the game, and basically that was it. I took a short vacation and was back in Farmington bagging groceries in a local supermarket. You heard me right, bagging groceries for whatever they would pay me. I wasn't allowed to work a 40-hour week because I wasn't a union member, but I would show up anyway on Saturdays if they were real busy so I could help out. The fact that I was a member of the New York Giants championship team meant nothing to anyone in Farmingdale.

Even though I had my credential to teach or coach, half the school year was already over. Those jobs had been filled in August while I was at camp. Mary was still working for John Manchin. I would work for him whenever he needed me. That extra paycheck sure came in handy. Football wasn't going to last forever; hell, it could come to a screeching halt at any time. I wanted a little money to fall back on.

The players of today sign huge contracts. Usually the first thing they do is go out and buy a brand new car. In '56 I bought a used, 1955, green Chevy. I'm sure most folks in Farmington thought I was making a lot of money playing football. Compared to everyone else in the town I was making a good salary, but I've always been somewhat tight with a buck. Maybe I should have been a little less frugal when purchasing a car.

We were renting a house in Farmington that was up on the top of a very steep hill. One day while Mary was driving down the driveway, she turned the wheel and the steering shaft literally broke. How she stopped that car I will never know. She could have been killed.

I continued to live in West Virginia during the off-season. Back in those days, there were no minicamps and no workout program. Lifting weights still hadn't made its mark in athletic training, so all we did was run or play basketball. You also had to make sure you didn't gain any weight during the off-season or you would hear it from the coach.

The only communication I ever received from the Giants prior to training camp was a contract that was sent to me in the mail. It usually arrived a month before camp commenced. There wasn't a lot of time to think about the contract, nor were the Giants willing to negotiate. All they wanted was for you to sign that piece of paper and mail it back to them as soon as possible.

When I saw the amount that was offered to me, I refused to sign it. Wellington had paid me $7,000 last year, and the contract for this year was for $7,500. A raise of only $500? I was insulted and felt I deserved better. So I sent the contract back, unsigned, and let Wellington know that I would discuss it when I got to camp.

Training camp was in Winooski, Vermont. Approximately two weeks into camp, Wellington initiated talks with me regarding my contract. We sat down in his office and he said, "Sam, we want you to sign this contract."

I explained to him that I wanted $8,500. He was furious. Next I told him that I would rather negotiate with his brother, Jack. Jack was in charge of the business side of the Giants and negotiated contracts with certain players.

Wellington told me, "Absolutely not! You can't talk to Jack because he has his favorite ballplayers and I sign all the tough guys."

He finally offered me $8,000, but I kept insisting that I wanted $8,500. All of a sudden Wellington became furious with me. His Irish temper was up. The veins in his neck began to protrude and his face turned scarlet. He stood up, grabbed all the papers on his desk and threw them all over the place. He leaned his hands on the desk, narrowed his eyes and looked directly into mine. With teeth clenched he said, "You will sign this contract or I'll trade you so fast you won't even know where you landed! Now you sign this contract!"

Sam Huff with his father, Oral Huff, and Sam's first son, Sam Huff Jr.

The entire Huff family.

Coach Steve Harrick's 1955 Mountaineer baseball team is as follows: First row, left to right: Jim Dobbins, Olan Carter, Bob Raines, John Baliker, Charlie McKown, Sam Huff, Don O'Haver, and Coach Harrick. Second row: Ed Lenart, Don Smith, Tom Cook, Glenn Higgins, Joe Geldbaugh, Ron Shafer, Phil Donley. Third row: Ronnie LaNeve, Rod Herman, Jim Baliker, Jim Heise, Vic Rabbits, Larry Kaltenecker. Fourth row: John Vehse, Christy Kaltenecker, Don Firestone, Jim Davoff, and Roy French.

1955 Mountaineer Baseball Team: Sam is 1st row, 3rd from the right.

Sam smiles as he charges the camera at the West Virginia University practice field in Morgantown. (Getty)

Sam Huff of the New York Giants. (AP)

Sam leaps the pile to chase down a play. (Getty)

NEW YORK GIANTS
1956 WORLD'S CHAMPIONS

1956 NEW YORK FOOTBALL GIANTS

First row: Ray Wietecha, Jim Patton, Herb Rich, Gene Filipski, Mel Triplett, Kyle Rote, Coach Jim Lee Howell, Bill Svoboda, Dick Modzelewski, Walt Yowarsky, Sam Huff, Gerald Huth, Dick Yelvington, Wellington Mara, Pete Previte.
Second row: John Johnson, John Dziegiel, Dick Nolan, Jack Stroud, Frank Gifford, Charley Conerly, Don Heinrich, Ray Beck, Ed Hughes, Roosevelt Brown Jr., Henry Moore, Harland Svare, Ed Kolman, Ken Kavanaugh, Pete Sheehy.
Third row: Em Tunnell, Bob Clatterbuck, Jim Katcavage, Andy Robustelli, Cliff Livingston, Alex Webster, Ken MacAfee, Roosevelt Grier, Bill Schnelker, Bill Austin, Don Chandler, Sid Moret, Tom Landry, Vince Lombardi.

The 1956 NFL Champion New York Giants. No. 70, Sam Huff is 1st row, 5th from the right.

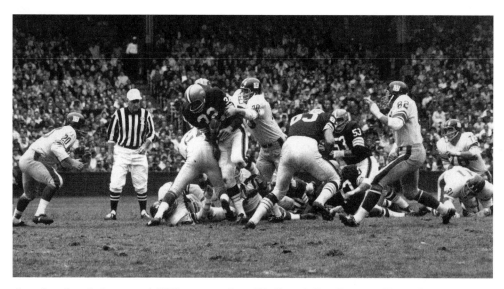

Another battle between NFL greats Sam Huff and Jim Brown. Here, Sam catches Brown from behind and drags him to the ground. (Getty)

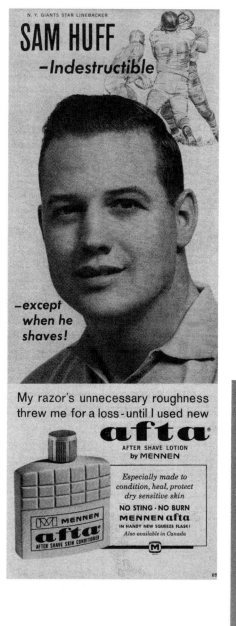

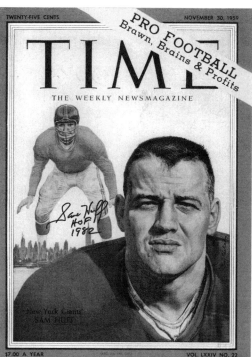

Sam in an ad for Afta After Shave (left) and on the November 30, 1959 cover of Time (right).

Huff and Taylor, one of the great rivalries in NFL history. Here, in September 1962, Sam wins, driving Taylor to the turf. (AP)

At 22, there was no doubt in my mind that I wanted to remain with the Giants. The team, my teammates, and playing before those huge crowds at Yankee Stadium was unparalleled. I decided to sign for $8,000. The extra $500 wasn't worth the wrath of Wellington.

Great Leading Men: Webster, MacAfee, Gifford, and Rote

Another guy you never wanted to see angry was our big, tough running back Alex Webster. Alex and I were good friends, but I would never, ever cross him. Webster liked to fight. When he lived in New Jersey he was known for street fighting. Alex scratched and clawed his way through life. His journey to the New York Giants wasn't an easy one. The Redskins drafted him out of North Carolina State and made him a defensive back. Just prior to the start of the 1953 season, he was cut. Alex decided to go to Canada and try out for the Canadian Football League. Not only did he make it, but he was the MVP in 1954. Al DeRogatis (who had seen me play at West Virginia) was still scouting for the Giants. He saw Alex playing for the Montreal Alouettes in Canada and convinced the Mara brothers that he was the big back they were looking for.

Webster joined us in 1955. In our first two exhibition games he scored three touchdowns. Howell liked him so much that he decided to start him at right halfback and move Kyle Rote to end.

By 1957 Alex had become a leader within the offensive unit. The offense and the defense had some brutal rivalries back then. In training camp many of the "friendly" rivalries would turn into blood wars. One year Wellington threatened not to give me a raise because he had witnessed five fights that I had been involved in. I told him, "Wellington, I never fought in five fights. It was only four."

The defense would completely annihilate the offense in practice. Not only did that piss off the offensive unit but Lombardi would totally lose it. He would scream and yell at the offense, and then as punishment he would keep the offense out on the field long after Landry released us to the showers.

One time the offense came into the locker room long after we already showered and dressed. We had an end by the name of Ken MacAfee. Ken was really nice and friendly to everyone, but his main fault was that he would always find a way to put his foot in his mouth.

As the offense dragged themselves into the sweltering locker room, you could see that they were in no mood for jokes. Lombardi had been on their ass all day.

Just then MacAfee yelled over to Alex, "You know, Webster, if you ever learned your plays, we wouldn't have to stay out there so long".

Alex was enraged. All of a sudden bodies were being thrown everywhere and lockers were crashing down all around us. Webster turned into a mad man and was working his way toward MacAfee. In the midst of it all, I was also knocked down. And if it weren't for the five guys who were able to restrain Webster, MacAfee would have been a dead man!

Another situation that occurred during training had to do with Frank Gifford. No one ever enjoyed training camp. It was a pain in the ass. The team would take you to these isolated places, away from the rest of the civilized world. We had two-a-day practices and then meetings the rest of the time. It was hell on earth. Then we were constantly on the road playing exhibition games, which no one really took seriously. We played half-heartedly to avoid injury prior to the start of the regular season. This usually resulted in an unsuccessful preseason for the Giants, and the 1957 campaign proved to be no different.

Anyway, it was late in the preseason and we had just lost a game in which both the offense and defense played terribly. All of a sudden Jim Lee Howell came into the locker room and just started blasting Frank Gifford.

Frank had worked his way up to NFL stardom. He seemed to have a storybook life. Gifford was the golden boy from the University of Southern California who married Miss California. He and his wife, Maxine, were the perfect couple. He was handsome and she was beautiful. They were seen regularly at Toots Shor's and P. J. Clarke's with all the who's who of the entertainment world. Frank even became a regular in the New York gossip columns.

He was a smart guy with goals in the business world. He knew exactly what he wanted and how he was going to get it. He worked his way into broadcasting and movies. I didn't think his acting was that great, but that's beside the point. Frank was a hustler and knew how to use his football career to open other doors. Even though we weren't what you would call close friends, I still considered him a friend, and I hope he would say the same about me. The one thing we did have in common was our mutual disdain for Jim Lee Howell.

Gifford had just finished an MVP season with the Giants, but Howell wasn't impressed in the least. He noticed that Frank had given a lackluster performance during the preseason, which was not uncommon for him or the rest of the offense. We had more than enough running backs who could play, so why not let the veterans kick back a little? Hell, you didn't want to give your all in August and have nothing left when the regular season began in September.

Anyway, we had been practicing at Fordham University. Each day following practice, the team would run laps around the field and then meet with Howell for one of his talks. It was at this point that he ripped into Frank.

"You guys were just terrible out there. You look like you've never played the game before. And then there's Mr. Hollywood, No. 16, the Most Valuable Player in the National Football League. Right now he is the worst player on this football team. He hunkers up (that was Howell's favorite expression) when he's supposed to be running with the ball."

You could have heard a pin drop. Frank was totally upset. He had tears in his eyes. The rest of us were not comfortable with it either. Jim Lee's remarks were totally uncalled for, and everyone knew it, especially Frank. Gifford was always the diplomatic type, but I believe he never forgave Howell for what he did to him. Everyone on that team knew that they could count on Gifford to make the big plays and be the star of the game.

Webster was another guy that Howell could not keep out of the starting lineup. As an athlete, Alex was in the worst shape of any player I'd ever seen. He had chronic ear infections and bad knees from all the hits he had taken. Worst of all, he was a chain smoker. He was the only guy I've ever seen smoking on the sidelines during a game. He would get under those huge capes we used to wear to keep warm, and puff away. You could always see the smoke bellowing out of the top of the cape.

But like Gifford, he always made the big plays. He may have been slow but when the team needed that third-and-one, Webster was the guy you could count on. If he was that good with all the problems he had, just imagine how great he could have been if he had taken care of himself combined with an extensive off-season conditioning program. With that madman temper of his there wouldn't have been an opponent in the NFL who could have controlled him on the field.

I made it my business to study the officials. It was important to know how and what they would call, to know each one's style of officiating. You also wanted to know how much you could get away with. Back in those days, I knew each and every one of them, even their wives' and kids' names. I made it a point to talk with them before, during, and after a game. Getting friendly with them was an edge in my favor because I always figured that if they knew you, they might think twice before throwing a flag on you for a penalty.

The captain of the offense was a guy by the name of Kyle Rote. Not only was he smart, but he was well-liked by everyone on the team. An All-American hero out of SMU, Rote was the first player taken in the 1951 draft. Kyle's downfall was that he had extensive knee problems. This chronic condition caused Lombardi to move him to end when Alex Webster joined the team.

Kyle was always a gentleman. He would drink, smoke, and play poker like the rest of the team but never in excess. He made such an impression on the players that it seemed like any time a boy was born to a player they would name him Kyle. Both Jimmy Patton and Frank Gifford named their sons Kyle. I used to joke to the guys and say that everyone named their sons after Kyle and their dogs after me.

Kyle was our captain and he took over the responsibilities that came with the job. For instance, if someone in the organization had a death in the family, Kyle would collect money from the players to cover the cost of flowers. He would make sure that everyone stepped up to the plate and did their part. Kyle made sure the locker boys were taken care of and collected the tip money for the college students who served meals at training camp.

The Giants had become a family. We celebrated holidays together and brought our kids to practice on Saturdays. And it was guys like Kyle Rote who took on the responsibility to continue that family atmosphere. To this day I believe it was one of the reasons for the Giants' continued success. For the first time, I felt as though I was part of something special.

Brown, Tittle, and the Alley-Oop

I wish I could have said the same about the 1957 Giants, but fate didn't plan it that way. We lost our first game to Cleveland then won our next three against Philadelphia, Washington, and Pittsburgh, only to lose to the Redskins in the fifth game of the season. It looked like we had gotten it together when we won four straight: Green Bay, Chicago, Philadelphia, and Chicago. We were on a roll and the division crown was practically ours. Then disaster hit. We lost our last three games to San Francisco, Pittsburgh, and Cleveland and finished second to the Browns. To add insult to injury, we lost to a Cleveland team with a rookie fullback out of Syracuse by the name of Jimmy Brown.

As incredible as it may seem, Jimmy wasn't the No. 1 pick of the draft that year. A Heisman Trophy-winning halfback out of Notre Dame named Paul Hornung was the No. 1 pick. As a matter of fact, Brown was chosen sixth overall, behind Hornung, Jon Arnett, John Brodie, Ron Kramer, and Len Dawson.

But I'd already been introduced to the speed, power, and strength of Jim Brown from my days at West Virginia, and before the Giants were to play our season opener against the Browns I enlightened and warned my teammates about this incredible fullback out of Syracuse University.

In our first game, as we had done in the past, we stayed with our 4-3 defense. But over the years, we had to change and acclimate to a different defense when playing Cleveland in order to stop Jim Brown.

Both the Browns and the Giants played an incredible defensive game, with neither allowing a touchdown all day. We even held Jim Brown to 89 yards on 21 attempts. It was a game of field goals, right down to the last seconds of the game.

The game was played at Cleveland's Municipal Stadium, and we scored first, with a 32-yard field goal by Ben Agajanian in the second quarter. A little later on in the game, Agajanian kicked another field goal which made the score 6–0, but the Browns were offsides and Howell decided to take the points off the board and go for the touchdown. The offense moved the ball to inside the 15-yard line, but this time Agajanian missed the kick and the score remained 3–0. Late in the second quarter, Lou Groza kicked a field goal to tie the game. Neither team was able to move the ball in the third, but in the fourth quarter, with only 21 seconds remaining, Groza kicked a 47-yard field goal to win the game. Final score: Cleveland 6, New York 3.

I learned two important lessons that day. First of all, never take points off the board because it will come back to haunt you, and second, I had to be at the top of my game any time I was going up against Jim Brown.

That same year my daughter, Cathy, was born. Since it was during the season, Mary stayed back in Farmington to have the baby, and I continued to live at the Grand Concourse with roommates Don Chandler and Bill Svoboda.

Another memorable event occurred in December of that year when the Giants played against the San Francisco 49ers in New York. Even though we lost that game by a score of 27–17, I made what some people consider to be the greatest tackle in the history of professional football.

49ers quarterback Y.A. Tittle dropped back eight yards and threw a screen pass to his star halfback Hugh McElhenny. As I looked upfield I saw McElhenny running behind my old college teammate, Bruce Bosley, along with another big guard by the name of Lou Palatella. The combined weight of the three of them totaled over 650 pounds and it was all coming down on me. The only thing I could think of was to remove the lead blocker and let someone else make the tackle. I ended up just popping into Boseley and Palatella. I hit both of them so hard in the chest that it knocked them both down and my momentum carried me right into McElhenny. All three went down like a ton of bricks, and the fans at Yankee Stadium went wild.

I attribute that loss to San Francisco on one play that was made famous between quarterback Y.A. Tittle and a 6'3" end by the name of R.C. Owens. R.C. was drafted out of the College of Idaho, where he also played basketball. The play was nicknamed the Alley-Oop. Tittle would drop back and lob the ball in R.C.'s direction. Being the tremendous leaper that he was, Owens would simply out-leap any defensive backs around him. He was almost impossible to stop.

The following week we played the Steelers in Pittsburgh. We lost that game to Earl Morrall and Company by a score of 21–10. Cleveland also lost the next day to Detroit, but they still replaced us as Eastern Division champions. But the fact that we fell to second place didn't matter to our fans. By midweek the organization had sold 50,000 tickets, which at that time was the largest advance sale in the history of the club. On gameday we drew the largest crowd of the season by playing in front of 54,000 cheering fans.

I can remember Landry telling us prior to the start of the game, "If you hold Jim Brown to four yards a carry, we'll beat Cleveland."

Now, it doesn't take a genius to figure out that if he gets four yards a carry, three downs multiplied by four yards in West Virginia math is still a first down. Hell, he averaged 5.2 yards a carry his entire career.

Anyway, we played a hell of a game that day. Even though we lost 34–28, the game was exciting right down to the end. With seconds left on the clock, we drove deep into Cleveland territory, but time ran out on us. Through it all, the New York fans never gave up on us.

Even though we placed a disappointing second in the division, the season wasn't a total loss. Because of Landry's defensive strategies directed at Jim Brown, I learned how to stop the big fullback and perhaps the greatest runner in NFL history. We held him to only one TD that day. My assignment was to stop Brown. I followed him wherever he went. That's how the Huff vs. Brown rivalry began.

The Greatest Back in the NFL

Jim Brown had every quality needed to be the greatest back in the NFL. He had size, speed, strength, and intelligence. At 6'2", 232 pounds, he always knew what to do and where to go. In order to conserve his strength, he would use his blockers. There were times when he would run straight up the middle and let you hit him, that is, if you could get a shot at him. He was so damn strong and fast that if he didn't run by you, he would run over you. Hitting him was like running into steel. There was no give to his massive physique. He would sometimes be gang-tackled by three or four Giants and just drag them to the goal line. There was no one like him, then or now.

Not only was Brown the greatest player I've ever seen, but he showed good sportsmanship on the field. He would actually compliment me after I'd hit him with everything I had. He would get up real slow and say, "Nice tackle, big Sam."

That's just the way he was.

On the other hand, Jimmy could make you look bad. I remember one game where I flew into a hole, hit him, and he continued to run for a 17-yard gain. When I returned to the sidelines, Landry asked me, "What happened? Were you late getting in the hole?"

"No, Tom," I said. "He just ran right over me."

Our defensive back, Dick Nolan, also experienced the wrath of Jim Brown. In one of our games against Cleveland their center got a hold on my ankle and I couldn't get back in time to fill the hole. Brown raced through and it was now up to Nolan to stop him. Dick weighed only about 175 pounds and was called Sticks by his teammates because he was so thin. Nolan hit Brown with everything he had and they both fell to the ground. Jim got right up, but Nolan didn't move. When I went over to help him up, his eyes had rolled back into his head.

"Great tackle, Dick," I said, somewhat uneasily. "I'm really sorry I didn't get there in time. Somebody picked me off."

He looked up at me, his eyes still not focused and said, "Great tackle, hell, Sam! I couldn't get out of that son of a bitch's way!"

1958: Defense! Defense!

We began the season with a 1–5 exhibition record then went on to lose two of our first four regular-season games. Who would have ever believed that we were Eastern title bound and about to play in what is now known as the Greatest Game Ever Played, the 1958 championship game between the New York Giants and the Baltimore Colts?

Despite our miserable preseason record, many of the players felt that Mara had acquired some great talent in the off-season, especially in the secondary. Dick Nolan and Bobby Joe Conrad were traded to the Chicago Cardinals in exchange for cornerback Lindon Crow and veteran kicker Pat Summerall. Rosey Grier had returned from active duty in the army after missing the previous season, and veteran defensive back Carl Karilivacz was sent to us from Detroit. Wellington drafted Vanderbilt fullback Phil King and a halfback out of Texas-El Paso by the name of Don Maynard. Maynard was cut after the '58 season, but was picked up by the New York Jets (Titans, at that time), moved to the wide receiver position, and became Joe Namath's No. 1 receiver. As a side note, Maynard was inducted into the Pro Football Hall of Fame in 1987. Don wore cowboy boots and spoke with such a thick, southern accent that none of us could understand a word he said.

As far as the defensive unit went, it was our third year under Landry and with Grier back in the middle, we knew we could dominate our opponents. On the other hand, the defense had to be good because our offense wasn't that strong. The entire season we averaged only 20 points a game. Our average margin of victory was approximately five points. Our new kicker, Summerall, was the primary scorer with 25 percent of our total points made on field goals and extra points.

Near the end of the decade our defense, with its brutality and vengeance, was not only becoming noticed, but was down right celebrated by the fans at Yankee Stadium. They would literally begin chanting Robustelli, Robustelli, Huff, Huff, or Defense, Defense. When I would hear that, chills would run up and down my spine, and I honestly feel that it made us play that much tougher. Sportswriters started to come up with key terms like "sanctioned savagery" or "vengeance with style." There may have been fewer rules in those days, but the game was far more exciting to watch and to play.

A Colorful Cast of Characters: Modzelewski, Grier, Katcavage, Robustelli, & Tunnell

At 6'1" and weighing only 255 pounds, Dick Modzelewski was one of the strongest people I've ever seen. He was impossible to move. His vision wasn't that great, so he wore contact lenses when he played. Regardless of his size and vision, Dick always got the job done. He was also a fun guy to be around. Take training camp, for instance. After finishing our calisthenics, Howell would have us run a couple of laps around the baseball diamond. On one side of the field there was an old wooden backstop that we would run around to complete a lap. Mo would hide behind the boards after the first lap. As the rest of us were huffing and puffing on our second lap, Mo would begin running and lead the entire team to the finish line, no huffing or puffing because he'd only completed one lap.

Jim Lee fell for it every time. He would yell to Mo, "Atta way to go, Mo, way to lead 'em in!"

We would all fall over laughing, but no one cared that Mo didn't run the two laps. That was his personality, and everyone enjoyed it.

Mo loved to eat, tell stories, and sing Polish folk songs. He hailed from a small town in the Pittsburgh area by the name of West Natrona. Every time the Giants would play the Steelers he would take some of guys over to his mother's house where they would devour these huge meals. When we played the Browns at Cleveland, Mo would take everyone to his brother Ed's restaurant. The food was terrific—so terrific that you would overeat and barely be able to move afterward.

Another big eater was Rosey Grier. As a matter of fact, his weight was one of the reasons the team traded him to the Rams in 1963. He had an uncontrollable eating disorder that skyrocketed his weight to 340 pounds in the off-season. During training camp, Rosey had to sit at the Weight Watchers' table where he could consume only salad and Jell-O. Not exactly the diet a man of that size could enjoy. At night he would sneak out of the facility and eat anything and everything he could get his hands on.

Grier was a talented player, and because of his speed he had the ability to catch opposing players from behind. But keeping in shape was not exactly his forte. He would consistently ask us to call timeout so he could catch his breath. But when he made up his mind to do something, like sacking the quarterback, there weren't too many people in the league who could stop him.

Some of his most intense battles happened not against opponents, but against his own teammates. Jack Stroud was one of our offensive linemen. He practiced weightlifting back when no one else was doing it. He was strong as hell, probably the strongest guy on the team. One day during practice, he and Rosey were going up against one another in the nutcracker drill. At the end of the day we were all the locker room and Rosey said to Jack, "You know, Stroud, when I play against you, I'm playing for my life."

Rosey was really a great guy and liked by everyone. Like Kyle Rote, Grier was always a gentleman. He loved to strum on the guitar, but couldn't play it worth a damn. One year during training camp, we were working out twice a day. We would be dead tired by nightfall. While we were all trying to get some sleep, Rosey would be strumming that guitar and pissing everyone off, but no one had the balls to tell him to stop playing.

The year after we moved our training camp to Fairfield, Connecticut, Rosey went out and bought an electric guitar, complete with amplifier. One day someone stole a tube out of his amp. The next day at lunch, Grier stood up and said in a calm voice, "Gentlemen, I want to tell you that somebody took the tube out of my amplifier. It better be returned tonight or I'm gonna take each guy, one at a time, and find out who did it."

Miraculously, that night, the tube found its way back into that amplifier.

Another character was our defensive end out of Dayton University, Jim Katcavage. Jim joined the team the same year as I did. He had more heart than any other football player I've ever seen. Whether we were practicing or in a game situation, Jim only knew one speed: all out.

One Thursday in 1963 we were practicing for our meeting with the Chicago Bears for the world championship. Our coach, Allie Sherman, had us work out in only helmets and shoulder pads. The offense was playing against the defense, and Sherman wanted us to go half-speed. Katcavage never knew what that meant, so when the ball was snapped he bowled his way through the line like a bat out of hell and crushed our quarterback Y.A. Tittle. Y.A.

had already been in the league for 15 years and was too old to be hit like that in practice. Sherman was not happy about the hit, and when we got back into our defensive huddle, I told Jim, "Kat, for God's sake, what the hell did you do that for? He's an old man, and we need him healthy on Sunday."

Jim looked over at me and said, "Sam, you don't understand. I have to battle that offensive tackle every day to get to the quarterback, every day. So I get through the line and he's standing there with the ball. What am I supposed to do? I've got to hit that quarterback."

I completely understood what he was saying. You never want to discourage that kind of aggression in a good defensive ballplayer because he'll always play to the best of his ability. I told Jim, "Kat, if you get through, just hit him. Go ahead and get him."

Back in 1959 we were playing the Eagles. Kat hated Philadelphia. He was from the area and wanted nothing more than to play well against his hometown team. On the first play of the game Jim broke through the hole and took on the Eagles' guard. In the process he broke his collarbone, which is one of the most painful of all injuries. He ended up playing three quarters with the injury. After having it X-rayed, he was told that he would be out for the rest of the season.

Our other end, Andy Robustelli, was more of an analytical player. As a matter of fact he replaced Landry as defensive coach when Tom left in 1960 to coach the new Dallas Cowboys franchise. He had been in the league since he had been drafted by the Los Angeles Rams in 1951. Robustelli possessed great strength and could always be counted on to make the big play when called upon. In the huddle, and on third-and-7, I remember him saying, "Okay, guys. We gotta get 'em right here!"

And I'll be damned if he didn't either sack the quarterback or block a field goal. He was always determined to get the job done.

Off the field, Andy had many irons in the fire, so many that we couldn't keep up with what he was doing from week to week. He owned a chain of sporting goods stores and travel agencies as well as a mail-order clothing line.

One time he talked the team into buying these beautiful cashmere sports coats that were tailored in Hong Kong. The only problem was that a large or extra-large in Hong Kong wasn't the same as a large or extra-large in the United States. The coats were all too small. I ended up giving my jacket to Bobby Epps, one of our smaller running backs, and it was too small even for him.

In 1960 when CBS was filming "The Violent World of Sam Huff," Andy, Kat, Mo, Rosey, and I all wore these striped shirts for the shoot courtesy of Robustelli. We got the free shirts and he got some free advertising.

In 1971 Andy was enshrined into the Pro Football Hall of Fame. As a matter of fact, three of us from our defensive unit were, at different times, inducted—Andy, me, and an incredible safety by the name of Emlen Tunnell.

Emlen's journey to the New York Giants is an even more incredible story. Upon graduating from Iowa in 1948, Emlen had gone undrafted because of an eye injury that he received during his senior year. But he was determined to play pro ball. He decided that he would hitchhike from his home near Philadelphia to the headquarters of the New York Giants organization. Upon arriving unannounced, he made his way to the Giants' offices looking for a job.

The team's general manager at that time was a guy by the name of Ray Walsh. He recognized Tunnell from his playing days at Iowa. Ray decided to invite him to camp.

From the time Emlen first stepped on the field, there was no doubt in anyone's mind that he belonged in the National Football League. He was outstanding on both offense and defense as well as on special teams as a punt and kickoff return man. Tunnell was also the first black player to be signed by the Giants. When his career as a player ended, he went on to become the first black assistant coach in the NFL. And later, in 1967, the first African American ever to be enshrined into the Pro Football Hall of Fame as a defensive player.

At that time, Emlen was considered by most to be the hardest hitter in the league. Receivers were in fear of their life when they were forced to catch a pass in front of him. At 6'1", 210 pounds he would hit them so damn hard that they'd be taken out of the game, sometimes permanently.

Emlen played football solely for the love of the game, and he considered it an honor to play for the Giants. The money was never an issue.

In 1975, Emlen died of a heart attack, and he died penniless. He literally gave away all his money to his friends. He was generous to a fault. When we would go out for a drink, he would not only buy you a round, but he would buy the *house* a round! He'd sometimes do this two to three times a night. By the time we closed the bar down, Emlen would leave without a cent in his pocket.

Later in his career, and while still with the Giants, Emlen's speed began to slow and he showed difficulty in understanding Coach Landry's defensive strategies. In 1959 the Giants asked him to retire, but Tunnell was financially strapped. He requested that he be put on waivers.

Vince Lombardi was now head coach of the Packers, and when he saw Emlen's name on the waiver list he immediately acquisitioned the future Hall of Fame defensive back. Lombardi also knew that Emlen's skills far exceeded those of any player he had at Green Bay at the time.

That same year, the Giants played a preseason game against the Packers in Bangor, Maine. Charlie Conerly threw a swing pass over the middle to our running back, Joe Morrison. Emlen, who was playing safety for the Pack, came up to Joe and hit him with a shot that could be heard all around the stadium. Joe was knocked out cold.

I also remember Jim Lee Howell's reaction to the hit. "Hey, Emlen! You never hit like that when you were with us!"

At that time, Wellington Mara was standing on the sidelines and heard Jim Lee's remark to Tunnell. Emlen was not only a favorite of Wellington's, but he was also a favorite of his father, Tim Mara, the original owner of the team. In all the years that I played for New York, I figure that I met Tim maybe 10 times. He could never even remember my name.

Just then Wellington angrily set his sights on Howell and said, "Jim Lee, don't you ever say that about Emlen! He played hard for you, and he was one of us. He was a great player and don't you ever put that knock on him again!"

Emlen was a major contributor to the 1958 Giants-Colts championship game. Sadly, as it turned out, it would be his last game in a Giants uniform.

That Incredible '58 Season

It's been 53 years since that incredible '58 season and it still amazes me that the Giants advanced as far as they did. By November 30 our record was 7–3 with two games still to go. The race to win the division was extremely close, with the Cleveland Browns holding an 8–2 record.

On Sunday, December 7, we played the Lions in Detroit in a must-win game in order to have a shot at the championship.

It was late in the third quarter and Detroit had taken the lead 17–12. But thanks to a huge mental error made by the Lions' coach, George Wilson, we were given a reprieve. The Lions were up by five and had possession of the ball. The only problem was that they were facing a fourth-and-21 at their own 44-yard line. The punting team took the field, but punter Yale Lary faked the kick and tried to run. Our defensive unit tackled Lary and allowed only a one-yard gain. Not only did the Giants have possession of the ball, but we were also in great field position. On the next play of the game, Conerly threw to Bob Schnelker for a 34-yard gain, and on fourth-and-2, handed the ball to Gifford who went in for the score. We had gone ahead 19–17, but there was still enough time left for one more score. With only seconds left in the game, Detroit set up for a field goal to win it. The ball was snapped, but the kick was blocked by Harland Svare. Final score: Giants 19, Lions 17.

Our final game of the regular season was against Cleveland. It was snowing that day and the cold was unbearable. Not only did we have to beat the Browns in this game to force a playoff, but we had to beat them a second time in order to play the Baltimore Colts for the championship.

On the first offensive play of the game, Jim Brown rushed for a 65-yard touchdown. That shook us up pretty good, but we regained our composure, and in the fourth quarter tied the game with Gifford throwing a halfback option pass to Schnelker for an eight-yard touchdown. The score was now tied at 10-all.

Our kicker Pat Summerall had been nursing a bad knee all week and was unable to practice. With four and a half minutes remaining in the fourth quarter, Pat missed a 31-yard field goal. But Summerall was granted one more chance.

Our defense was able to stop Cleveland on three consecutive Ed Brown passes and regained possession at midfield. On second down, with time running out, Conerly hit Alex Webster at the 5-yard line, but Alex dropped the ball. Two plays later, Jim Lee Howell called a play that not only shocked the entire stadium, but the Giants as well.

The snow was now coming down hard and heavy. The chalk lines could no longer be seen and visibility had dwindled down to about two feet. That's when Howell decided to send out the field goal unit to try a 49-yard kick. No one was more surprised than Summerall.

The ball was snapped and Pat miraculously kicked it straight through the uprights. We beat the Browns 13–10, and both teams' records were now tied at 9–3. The Giants would have to play Cleveland one last time for the divisional playoff.

December 21 finally arrived and we met the Browns on our home field at Yankee Stadium in front of a capacity crowd. That day we showed our best defensive effort against Jim Brown, holding him to only eight yards rushing on 12 carries. We ended up holding the entire Cleveland offense to a total of only 86 yards.

I remember this one play where Jimmy took a pitchout and slipped on the icy ground. Just as he was about to hit the frozen field, Mo hit him low and I hit him high. I thought we knocked him out, but to this day he attests that he never was knocked out because he never stayed down after the hits.

Our only touchdown was scored on a trick play. It began as a double reverse—a handoff to Webster going left from Conerly, and another handoff to Gifford around the right end—but just as Frank was about to be smacked by the Browns' defense he pitched the ball back to Conerly, who ran it in for six points. In the second quarter, Summerall kicked a field goal. That made the score 10–0. Those 10 points were all we needed to clinch the Eastern title. Final score: Giants 10, Cleveland 0. Next stop: the championship game against the relentless Baltimore Colts.

The Greatest Game Ever Played

We knew we were in for a battle against the league-leading Colts. With guys like Unitas, Berry, Moore, and Ameche on offense, and Marchetti, Donovan, and Lipscomb on defense, you knew that it was going to be a long afternoon. It would be the classic confrontation of offense vs. defense.

Just before the game, Landry said, "The score is seven to nothing, and we haven't even kicked off yet!"

It was inevitable that the Colts would score on us, and even the smallest of mistakes could cost us the game.

As fate would have it, Gifford fumbled twice by the second quarter. As we dragged ourselves to the locker room at the end of the half, the score read: Colts 14, Giants 3.

Only a few minutes into the third quarter, Unitas had moved his team all the way down to the Giants 3-yard line where it was now first-and-goal. But in the Giants' huddle, we were determined not to let them score on us. Ameche took a handoff from Unitas and ran to the 1. On second down, Unitas tried a quarterback sneak on us, but we had his number, and immediately hit him. On third down, it was once again Ameche, but Rosey Grier and I stopped him cold. On fourth down, Unitas thought we would be expecting Ameche up the middle, so instead, he threw him a pitch out to the right side where Cliff Livingston tackled him for a four-yard loss and the Giants' offense regained possession of the ball.

Now it was our turn. It was third-and-2 on our own 13-yard line. Conerly faked a pitch to Gifford, then threw to Rote, who was wide open over the middle. Kyle ran all the way to the 25, but had the ball stripped from him as he was caught from behind. Luckily for us, Alex Webster was right behind him, scooped up the ball and ran it down to the 1. Our fullback, Mel Triplett, charged it in for the score. We were back in the game with only a four-point differential. In the fourth quarter, Conerly hit Gifford for a 15-yard score, and Summerall's conversion gave us a 17–14 lead. But as long as there was time left on the clock, you could never underestimate the genius of Unitas.

Late in the final quarter, Unitas, on second-and-6 at our 27-yard line, was hit and sacked by Andy Robustelli. Andy had beat future Hall of Fame tackle

Jim Parker and just smacked Unitas for an 11-yard loss. Mo then hit him for a nine-yard loss. It was now fourth-and-26, and the Colts had no alternative but to punt. All we needed was a couple of first downs to win our second NFL title in the past three years. But the powers that be had something else in mind, something that would change the course of professional football forever.

The series started with a 10-yard pass from Conerly to Webster, but on third-and-4 at our own 40, the game changed. Gifford took a handoff from Conerly, and while running wide to the right he was tackled by Gino Marchetti. As the two of them hit the field, Big Daddy Lipscomb jumped on the pile. In doing so, Lipscomb shattered Marchetti's ankle. It was obvious that Marchetti was in great pain, and throughout the entire ordeal, the ball was spotted about six inches short of the first down. The referee actually moved the ball back! I have viewed those game films over and over, and there is no doubt in my mind that Gifford made a first down.

Jim Lee now had to decide whether to go for the first down or to punt. He chose to punt, and why not? We had the lead; we had Don Chandler, the best punter in the league; and we had the greatest defense in the entire NFL. The Colts couldn't actually count on their kicker, Steve Myhra, to get the job done if called upon. He had completed only 4 of 10 field-goal attempts all year. There was no question in my mind that Howell made the right decision.

Chandler's punt landed on the Colts 14-yard line. Unitas threw two incomplete passes and it was now third-and-10. In classic Unitas form, he hit Lenny Moore for 11 yards, keeping the drive alive.

On the next two plays, Unitas hit Berry for a 25-yard gain and a 15-yard gain, both up the middle. Karilivacz was covering Raymond both times, but failed to make the play. On first down at the Giants' 35-yard line, Unitas went to Berry a third time for a 22-yard gain to the 13-yard line. John Unitas had moved his team 62 yards, and still had time for Myhra to kick the game-tying field goal. Much to everyone's surprise, Steve boomed a 20-yarder straight through the uprights to tie the game and send it into overtime.

No one knew what to expect. This was the first championship game to ever end in a tie. We were about to embark on a completely new facet of professional football, a rule appropriately named Sudden Death. Sudden Death is exactly what the name implies. It means that the first team to score within the allotted time is the winner and the losing team is, well, suddenly dead.

Unitas called tails on the coin toss. It came up heads and the Giants elected to receive. We couldn't seem to do anything right. Maynard bobbled the ball on the opening kickoff. Luckily for us he was able to recover it and bring it out to the 20-yard line. Conerly took over, but was unable move the team downfield, so Chandler came in to punt.

The next 13 plays confirmed the ice-in-his-veins legend of Johnny Unitas. Remarkably, Johnny moved the Colts 80 yards in those 13 plays.

Unitas and Company took over at their own 20-yard line. Twice we pushed Unitas back into third-and-long situations, and twice he found receivers Ameche and Berry open. The Colts now had a first down at the Giant 43-yard line. This would be the beginning of the end for the Giants.

Next, Unitas called a trap play. He handed off to Ameche, who ran 23 yards up the middle to the New York 20. Four plays later the Colts were on the 7-yard line. On the following play, Unitas stepped back and threw to end Jim Mutscheller, who carried the ball to the 1.

With third-and-goal at the Giants' 1. Unitas called "16 power," a play designed to send Ameche through the right side of the line. Mutscheller and Moore just leveled our linebacker Cliff Livingston and our safety Emlen Tunnell. Colts tackle George Preas and guard Alex Sandusky cleared out a huge hole that the 220-pound Ameche roared through, literally falling from his momentum after crossing the goal line for the score, the game, and the title. This play would become one of the most famous NFL photos of all time, and would rightfully take its place in the annual of professional football.

It's since been called the Greatest Game Ever Played. First of all, you had one of the greatest offensive units going up against one of the most dominant defenses in the history of the game. Second, there were a record number of Hall of Fame players on both sides (12). For the Colts there were: Raymond Berry, Jim Parker, Johnny Unitas, Lenny Moore, Gino Marchetti, and Art Donovan. The Giants were represented by: Roosevelt Brown, Frank Gifford, Andy Robustelli, Emlen Tunnell, Don Maynard, and me.

It's also the first time a championship game had been decided by a sudden death overtime period. More than 50 million people watched the game on national television. It would turn out to be *the game* that would put professional football on the map.

Was it really the Greatest Game Ever Played? I would have to say, yes, but when the 1958 championship game had ended, sadly, it was gone forever. However, it will always be remembered as one of the great moments in NFL history.

1959: The Organization Begins To Change

The loss of the 1958 championship game was a mere memory for us when we headed out to training camp in Winooski for the start of the 1959 season. But when training camp was over and we returned to New York, the media capital of the world, the loss of the championship game was as clear to New Yorkers as if it were played yesterday.

Some extremely significant and newsworthy changes had developed within the Giants' organization. One of the major changes had to do with the coaching staff. Vince Lombardi was supposed to take over Jim Lee's head coaching position with the Giants following the end of the 1960 season. Howell, however, had decided that he wouldn't retire at that time. Lombardi was then offered the head coaching position with the struggling Green Bay Packers. He chose to go with the Packers, leaving the Giants assistant coaching position open.

With Vince gone, Wellington Mara decided to hire Allie Sherman as the offensive coordinator to replace Lombardi. Sherman had been an offensive assistant with the Giants prior to accepting a head coaching position in 1954 with the Canadian League. Allie had been credited with converting Charlie Conerly from a college tailback to a T-formation quarterback. As much as I despise this man for trading me to the Washington Redskins in 1964, I have to admit that he was an innovator in the game of football. Not only was he an outstanding offensive coordinator, but he was also the first coach to put men in motion on offense to confuse the defense. Like Lombardi and Landry,

Jim Lee Howell saw intelligence in Sherman's offensive strategies and gave him full reign with the offensive unit.

On defense our linebacker and defensive captain, Bill Svoboda, decided to retire after the 1958 season and was replaced in the lineup by one of our great special teams players, Cliff Livingston.

Cliff came to the Giants in 1954 out of UCLA. He was one more screwball that the coaching staff had to tolerate because he was such a talented player. Hailing from California, some of the guys thought that maybe Cliff was gay. I mean, hell, everyone in the league was wearing crew cuts, but not Cliff. He sported long, blond hair that was perfectly combed back, like that of a movie star, and he wore really tight jeans. He had that California beach tan and didn't walk like the rest of us. He strutted.

We found out quickly that Cliff was not gay. In fact, he loved women and they loved him. But Jim Lee Howell was not quite sure how to handle Livingston.

Being a good ol' boy from Arkansas, Jim Lee was constantly on Cliff's back. But because of his talent, Howell made exceptions for Livingston. Actually, Cliff was one of the first special teams specialists. On punts he was able to get to the punter and block the kick because he was so fast and agile. After the 1958 season, Cliff also played backup linebacker.

Livingston managed to get in a lot of playing time on the field; and he didn't do too badly off the field, either. I remember this one time when we were scheduled to play an exhibition game in Hershey, Pennsylvania. After the game we spent the night at one of the local hotels in town. Howell never made any formal announcement regarding bed check, so of course, we all went out—including Cliff—but when we all returned to the hotel early the next morning, Cliff was not among us.

Cliff, like the rest of us, knew that we had to catch a plane to Dallas in the morning for an exhibition game against the Colts. Then, in the wee hours of the morning, Livingston's roommate, Tom Scott, received a phone call from Cliff. "Hey, Tom. Pack my suitcase for me. I'll meet the bus at the Harrisburg airport."

Tom did just as Cliff had asked him.

When the bus pulled up in Harrisburg, Cliff was there to meet us. As he stepped onto the bus, not a word was said, not even from Jim Lee. Our plane finally arrived in Dallas. We were scheduled to be there for one week. Cliff had been injured in the game in Hershey and Howell didn't want to risk him getting hurt prior to the start of the regular season. On the day of the Colt game, Jim Lee gave us all his usual instructions and postgame itinerary. Following his spiel he looked over at Cliff and said, "Now, Livingston, you're not going to play tonight, and you better not break curfew and you better not miss that bus!"

Whenever Jim Lee told Cliff not to do something (off the field), it was like daring him to do it. Following the game, Cliff and a few of the players went out and met some stewardesses. After a night of drinking and partying, the guys returned to the hotel—that is, all except Cliff.

The following morning Cliff was still AWOL, and Jim Lee waited for no one. We left for the airport without him.

When we arrived at Love Field, the plane was waiting for us. Just then a beautiful woman came over to the bus, knocked on the door, and asked for Tom Scott. She told Tom, "Cliff is out in the car and he doesn't have any clothes. Do you have his suitcase?"

Before Tom could answer, Cliff bolted from the car and ran onto the plane, wearing only a bathing suit. He didn't have anything else on, not even shoes. Jim Lee was not at all amused. As a matter of fact, he fined Cliff and had him apologize to the entire team at the meeting. No one ever again had any doubts regarding Cliff's sexual preference.

1959 was also the year that the Giants had a surplus of quarterbacks. In addition to Charlie Conerly and Don Heinrich, the organization had traded to get quarterback George Shaw from the Colts. On top of that, our No. 1 college draft pick that year was a quarterback out of Utah by the name of Lee Grosscup.

And with all this controversy building up, wouldn't you know it, Gifford decided that he was ready for a change of position. You guessed it, he wanted to play quarterback. I guess he figured that since he played the position in high school and for two years at the University of Southern California, he would do well. After all, no one ran the halfback option as well as Gifford, and he did have a good arm. But in the back of my mind, I couldn't help but think, "Is this just one of Frank's publicity stunts?"

Jim Lee decided to let Frank try the position. As a matter of fact he played an entire half against the Lions during preseason. But he didn't have the fluidity or smoothness of a confident quarterback. In the second half one of our players became injured and Frank had to go back to playing halfback. That was the last we saw of Gifford at the helm.

When classes would commence at St. Michaels in Winooski, the Giants would pack up their belongings and relocate training camp to nearby Bear Mountain for the remainder of the preseason. In 1959 one of our preseason games landed on the Friday night just prior to the big Labor Day weekend. Before the game, Jim Lee told everyone that we could leave after the game on Friday and not have to return to camp until the following Monday night at eight o'clock. I was one of those guys who really got homesick, and was happy to be going home to West Virginia for a long weekend with my family.

We ended up losing the Friday night game and Jim Lee wasn't exactly pleased with our performance. In fact, he was so angry that he told the team that we were to return by Sunday at eight o'clock instead of Monday at eight. I'd be damned if I was going to cut short my vacation with my family. I worked it out with Mel Triplett to pick me and a few of the other guys up in his car in Pittsburgh. Mel would be driving back from Toledo, Ohio which wasn't that far out of his way.

As fate would have it, Mel got a late start Monday. He, like the rest of us, was afraid of Jim Lee and realized that if he stopped in Pittsburgh to pick us up, we would all be late. Therefore, he just drove straight through Pittsburgh without ever picking us up. After waiting a couple of hours for him to show and finally realizing that he would be a no show, we decided to rent a car and drive to Bear Mountain ourselves.

Things didn't go as smoothly as we had planned. We ended up getting lost in the mountains of upstate New York and didn't arrive in Bear Mountain till after two in the morning. We not only missed Howell's curfew, but also his once in a blue moon bed check!

The following day at our pre-practice meeting, Jim Lee started in on us. "Now some of the boys didn't get back in time last night, so they will each be fined $75 apiece."

Making only $9,000 a year, I wasn't about to give up $75. I was furious! So, right then and there, right on the practice field I told Jim Lee just how I felt. "I'll tell you what Jim Lee. I'll hold that $75 in my hand, and by God, I want to see you take it away from me!"

Jim Lee just looked me square in the eye and said, "We'll just see about that."

"Yes sir!" I yelled back. "We'll just see about that because you're not going to be able to take it away from me."

It had become a face-off between Howell and me, but neither one of us was about to back down.

Back in those days, the Giants had formed a player committee that would hear out our problems regarding the coaching staff and/or management, and try to resolve them before they escalated. I appeared before the committee that same night and gained everyone's sympathy. By that evening I'd cooled off some and realized that I had made a big mistake by challenging Howell's authority.

The committee had asked me if I would compromise and pay only $50 instead of the original $75. I agreed. Jim Lee also agreed, but in reality, he could have thrown me off the team for good, and there would have been no recourse whatsoever for me.

As I look back on that ordeal, I was pretty cocky to think that I could get away with such a bold move. Like everyone else on that team, I was expendable. And like everyone else on that team, I was always only one injury away from being cut. Thankfully, I was never seriously injured while playing for the Giants.

We opened up the 1959 season against the Rams in Los Angeles. That year L.A. had an exceptional team, including two incredible running backs: Ollie Matson and Jon Arnett. Matson, who came from the Chicago Cardinals, was traded to the Rams for an NFL-record nine players. He was also a 1952 Olympic medal winner in track. Jim Lee told Chandler that it didn't matter who received the ball on the kickoff. Both receivers were extremely dangerous and either one could run it all the way for a touchdown.

Luckily for us, the score at the end of the second quarter was 17–7 with Schnelker and Gifford scoring touchdowns and Summerall adding a field goal. The only score for the Rams was made on a two-yard rush by Ollie Matson. Los Angeles went ahead at the end of the third quarter 21–17, but it was Pat Summerall who scored two field goals in the fourth to win the game. Final score: Giants 23, Rams 21.

We played our second game against the Eagles in Philly and allowed them to score 49 points. As it turned out (and I'm not saying that the Eagles didn't play a better game than us, because they did), one of our scouts was quoted in the newspaper as saying that Philadelphia "wasn't much." Any team that reads unfavorable press about themselves is bound to take it out of the team who said it. And believe me, the Eagles really stuck it to us. Final score: Philadelphia 49, Giants 21. But our defense would make amends by winning 9 of our next 10 games.

The Defense Makes Its Mark and *Time* Comes Calling

Our defense was becoming more and more popular as the chanting of *Deeefense! Deeefense!* and *Huff! Huff! Huff!* became more and more intense. Our pictures appeared in the newspapers more than those of the offense. I can remember Gifford walking by a locker-room photo shoot and saying, "That's okay, guys, you get your face in the paper and I'll make all the money."

Toots Shor just loved us and when we would walk into his club he would come up to us and say, "I loooove the defense, I loooove the defense!"

We were celebrities in our own right and were treated as such by stars like Jackie Gleason, Frank Sinatra, and Ed Sullivan. It was a wonderful time to be a New York Giant and it was about to get even better.

Coming off the field after a victorious win, the Giants' locker room was overcome by sportswriters and reporters trying to get interviews and stories from the players. As I stepped out of the shower, a man, unfamiliar to me, came up and introduced himself as a writer with *Time Magazine*. He told me that *Time* was interested in doing a cover story on me.

Not being that familiar with the content of *Time*, I asked the reporter how much they were going to pay me for the interview. Hell, if I was good enough to be on the cover, I was good enough to get paid.

The reporter responded with, "Sam, it's a great honor to be on the cover. We don't pay people. We've had presidents and prime ministers on the over, and we've never paid anyone."

"Well, then I guess you won't be doing a story on me," I answered.

"Look, Sam, we're gong to have someone paint a portrait of you and I can guarantee you it will be one of the biggest things that ever happens in your lifetime."

The idea of a football portrait of me did catch my interest. I told him I would make a deal with him, "If *Time* would give me that portrait, I will agree to the story."

"I can't do that Sam. These portraits are to be hung in the boardroom at the Time/Life Building in Manhattan."

I reiterated. "No picture, no story."

The reporter told me that he would talk to his superiors and let me know. A couple of days later the reporter called back and we had a deal.

The weeks to follow were incredible. I was constantly surrounded by reporters and researchers and my phone was ringing off the hook. I was elated when the magazine finally hit the newsstands.

Not only was the story terrific, but the portrait was magnificent. That reporter was right about being recognized by *Time* and the impact it had on my life. To this day, I still receive copies of that magazine in the mail from fans requesting an autograph.

The article appeared on November 30, 1959, and was titled *Pro Football, Brawn, Brains, & Profits*. The following are two excerpts from the story.

The four blue-jerseyed men facing him are mountains of muscle. Alert and agile as jungle cats, two linebackers crouch outside the ends. Ranged in an arc behind them are four whippet-fast backs. And a mere two-yards away from the quarterback, returning his stare in challenge, waits the key main of the proud New York Giant defense—middle linebacker Sam Huff (6 ft. 1 inc., 230 lbs) a confident, smiling fighter fired with a devout desire to sink a thick shoulder into every ball carrier in the National Football League...

Huff [said] *"You play as hard and as vicious as you can. You've got more chance to get hurt when you're loafin'. You rap the quarterback every chance you get. He's the brains of the outfit. If you knock him out clean and hard on that first play of the game, that's an accomplishment. For that matter, we try to hurt everybody. We hit each other as hard as we can. This is a man's game."*

Getting Ready For The Colts

In our final 10 games of the season we lost only one, and that was to the Steelers. We also allowed only 100 points to be scored—an average of 10 points per game. We finished the '59 season 10–2–0 and were once again the NFL Eastern Division champs. The championship game would again be played against the NFL Western Division champs, the Baltimore Colts, who finished the season with a 9–3–0 record.

About this time, Mary was due with our third child. When she delivered Cathy in 1957, she had experienced some internal bleeding problems. With me being in New York for the championship, we rented a home in Flushing and Mary stayed with me. I wanted her in the big city because I felt that the medical care here would be far more advanced than what we had back home.

After informing the doctor in New York of her bleeding problem and the fact that I was at practice all day, he thought it would be best to induce labor. We scheduled Mary for the procedure.

The morning that the baby was to be born, I drove Mary to the hospital, dropped her off, and went to practice. I felt I could be with her after practice was over. In those days, fathers weren't allowed in the delivery rooms. But then, I wouldn't go in if they were allowed. I had trouble with giving blood, much less observing a surgery.

Concentrating on football was my main priority. I know that sounds somewhat cold-hearted, but that was how it was back then. You weren't allowed to take days off from practice. That was the rule. For instance, Andy Robustelli was playing for the Los Angeles Rams when his wife gave birth. Andy wanted to spend time with the two of them instead of reporting to training camp. The next thing he knew, he was traded to the Giants.

So I dropped Mary off, the doctors induced labor, and our son J.D. was born. There was only one problem, though, Mary's uterus had burst and she almost bled to death. With time of the essence, the doctors didn't have an opportunity to call me. An emergency hysterectomy was performed along with an injection of five pints of blood.

When I arrived home from practice that day, our sitter told me that I was needed at the hospital immediately. When I arrived, I was informed that the baby was fine, but Mary was in bad shape, barely alive. Her recovery was a long one and I truly believe that giving birth in New York instead of West Virginia saved her life.

The 1959 Championship Game

We went into that championship game with a great deal of confidence; and why not? Charlie Conerly led the NFL in passing and was the league's MVP; our kicker, Pat Summerall, finished second in scoring; our defense was rated No. 1 in the league, with me being voted the defensive MVP.

Coach Landry was more concerned with containing Johnny Unitas, Raymond Berry, and Lenny Moore, the same three who had beaten us the year prior. Tom also made the decision to single-cover Moore and double-cover Berry and the tight end, Jim Mutscheller. Landry explained it as, "We decided to concede a touchdown to Lenny Moore and cover him with only one man. This way we would be giving them their strength, hoping to cut off everything else. If our defense worked I figured we might win, 17–14 or 21–17."

The cornerback who was assigned to Moore was Lindon Crow. That poor son of a bitch. There was no way he could stop Lenny, but Landry was so damn stubborn that he refused to change his defense. He was famous for saying, "You're a professional. You play against the best and you're supposed to be the best, so you've got to figure out a way to cover!"

Bottom line: Lindon got burned all day, and it eventually cost us the game.

The game started off well for us; we led 9–7 though the third quarter. That nine points came on three Summerall field goals. Late in that same quarter we got a little momentum going and began driving downfield. We had a first down at the Colt 38, then came a fourth-and-1 situation on the 29. Last year during our championship game against Baltimore, Gifford was stopped short on third-and-inches. Instead of going for it, we did the "safe" thing and punted to the Colts. They rallied and sent the game into overtime. This time Howell took a gamble and went for the first down.

Conerly handed off to Alex Webster. In one of the few times in his career, Webster was stopped short by a pack of Baltimore defenders. Like the championship game of 1958, it was the beginning of the end for the Giants.

With Unitas at the helm, the Colts scored 24 points in the fourth quarter. Jimmy Patton was knocked out of the game with a foot injury and Lindon Crow took a knee to the face, compliments of Lenny Moore. At this point, Unitas was unstoppable.

Final score: Colts 31, Giants 16. Our defense may have been better than theirs, but our offense couldn't compete. That year Unitas set an NFL record with 32 touchdown passes.

The train ride back to New York was dismal and depressing. Not only had we lost a second championship to the Colts, but word had leaked out that Tom Landry would become the head coach of the expansion Dallas Cowboys team next season. With the loss of both Landry and Lombardi, the Giants were eventually doomed to fail.

Call for Philip Morris!

During the off-season of that year, I was called on to work for the Philip Morris Tobacco Company. Five Giants were chosen to represent the cigarette mogul: Chandler, Crow, Modzelewski, Patton, and I. Our respective territories were the areas we lived in.

It was a great job. We all received a company car, an expense account, and $250 a week to work our territories and meet and greet with wholesalers and retailers. We were guest speakers at the local Kiwanis and Rotary clubs and handed out free samples of Philip Morris cigarettes. Could you imagine doing that in today's world? Special interest groups would be all over you.

The irony of it all was that here I was working for a cigarette company, handing out free samples, making television commercials for their product, and I never smoked in my life. But they didn't care, and if it didn't matter to them, it sure didn't matter to me!

Like I had said before, it was a great job, but because of this job, I ended up taking the boat trip from hell.

Someone at Philip Morris thought it would be a great idea if we took the little bellhop (from the Philip Morris ads, you remember? "Call for Philip Morris") and brought him on a promotional boat trip down the intracoastal waterway which flowed from New York to Florida. Big mistake! The second day he got seasick and they had to find a substitute. Another genius thought it would be an even better idea to replace the "little guy" with a New York Giant, and that Giant was me.

As I boarded the boat, I had the misfortune of meeting the captain. Never have I met such a mean son of a bitch in my life. He was a retired admiral and treated his passengers as if they were crew members. Regardless what the agenda was for the day, when we docked we always had to return to the boat in the evening because everyone slept on board. But this piss-poor excuse for a captain would get everyone up by 5:00 AM to work on the vessel.

When we finally reached our south-most destination, I got off the boat as fast as I could. All of us were supposed to take that same boat with that crazy captain back up north. Not this guy. I boarded the first flight back to New York.

The Violent World of Sam Huff

"Today you will play pro football, riding on Sam Huff's broad back. We've wired him for sound with a tiny transistorized radio transmitter. It's not allowed in regular league play and it's the first time it has been done on television. The transmitter is embedded in his pads—the microphone goes in front. You're on the receiving end, and you're going to be closer to pro football than you've ever been before. This is our story: The Violent World of Sam Huff."

Walter Cronkite spoke those words on network television on the evening of October 31, 1960. It was broadcast as an episode of the Cronkite anthology series, *The Twentieth Century*. Many people believe that this dramatic introduction brought professional football out of the backwaters and into the mainstream of American sports.

"The Violent World of Sam Huff" was a life-changing event for me. It brought more recognition to me and to the linebacker position than I could have ever imagined.

The project was the brainchild of a CBS producer by the name of Burton Benjamin. He wanted to produce a documentary on professional football, but from a much different approach. Benjamin was more interested in a story about a contemporary figure than in the usual historical aspect of the sport. When I was approached about the project, I was elated. They paid me $500 and rented a car for me while they filmed at training camp.

The different approach that Benjamin had been talking about was the fact that I would be wired for sound. This had never been done before and CBS felt that the audience would have a real feel for the game of professional football. Ideally, Benjamin wanted me wired in a regular-season game, but the administration was resistant to allow it. They finally compromised, and allowed me to be wired in an exhibition game.

The film was broken down into three segments. The first segment was filmed back home in West Virginia. It showed me walking across my high school football field. My first lines were, "Any time that you play football there is no place for nice guys. I mean you have to be tough—you have to go all out. I always feel real good when I hit someone…you feel that you've accomplished something, you've made a beautiful tackle, and when we're out on that field we have to shake 'em up. It's either kill or be killed."

And later in front of the coal mine where my dad worked, "As a kid, I was raised in a coal-mining camp. Coal mining is all I have ever known, ever since I was a youngster. It's a very dangerous occupation and I'd rather take my chances on a football field. As long as I can play football, I'm going to stay out of there."

The final two segments were filmed during practice. The second part included the coaches and the players. Jim Lee Howell really played up the nice guy role. He made it look like he was the players' best buddy. Another scene showed Modzelewski singing a Polish folk song and Rosey Grier strumming his guitar. Our new defensive coach Harland Svare was shown diagramming plays in the classroom and questioning Jimmy Patton, Cliff Livingston, and me.

While all of this was going on, Walter Cronkite continued to give the nation an inside glimpse of the game of professional football.

"Pro football is really a collection of specialized trades. There are passing specialists, like Charlie Conerly; pass catching experts; men who only punt, men who only place-kick. Perhaps the middle linebackers like Sam Huff capture the imagination because they are rovers, masters of the red dog and the blitz, able to dart backward to cover the short pass zone, able to move in to fill a gap in the line.

"Finally, the end of the day. The hot shower will sting a dozen places where the skin is scraped away. There's a meal ahead and you may not be able to swallow, a two-hour conference and 22 plays to learn by morning. Yet this is only the beginning, a prelude to the big games to come, when the leather really begins to thud. That's when the world of Sam Huff becomes most violent, and that's the world we have wired for sound."

The third and final segment of the project was filmed while we were playing the Chicago Bears in a preseason game in Toronto. I was wired with a mike and a small transmitter that was inserted into my shoulder pads. Early in the game Bears receiver Harlon Hill really put a hit on me long after the whistle had blown. I stood up and said to him, "Harlon, for god sake you never hit anyone in your life! What the hell did you do that for?"

"Aw, Sam," he said. "I just wanted to get on TV."

That seemed to be the attitude of all the Bears players. Hit Huff and you'll get on TV!

Harlon's hit was cut from the project, but end Willard Dewveall's cheap shot wasn't. Dewveall clobbered me with a forearm under my face mask. My first response to him was bleeped out, but this wasn't.

"Whaddya do that for, 88? You do that one more time, 88, and I'm gonna sock you one. You do that again and you'll get a broken nose. Don't hit me on the chin with your elbow. Hey, 88, I'm not gonna warn you no more now."

I wasn't about to give Dewveall the satisfaction of hearing his name on television, and that's why I consistently referred to him as "No. 88."

After the show aired, the entire nation was talking about it. I received hundreds of letters from all over the country. The airing came at a time when pro football was beginning to get the attention it deserved.

But there was also a negative side to all this. Many players, including my own teammates, were envious of me. I didn't ask for this. CBS came to me. With New York being the media capital of the nation I guess they felt that the Giants were the team to film. Dave Kindred, a writer for *The Washington Post*, had this to say about the project: "Some may have thought the extraordinarily graphic film—never had we seen this war up close and personal—raised Huff's fame to heights disproportionate to his ability."

For years I would hear people say I was a media creation, and that every time sports announcer Chris Schenkel called the play-by-play when our defense was out on the field, he would say, "Huff makes the tackle."

Let me tell you something, I made a lot of tackles because that's the way Tom Landry designed our defense. Do you expect me to apologize? Hell no! This was all part of a team concept, and my teammates accepted that.

Some even began to portray me as the villain of the NFL. When we would play other teams away, the press would have a field day writing stories about how overrated I was. They would say things like, "Wasn't it a shame they didn't do The Violent World of Bill George, or Joe Schmidt or Ray Nitschke?"

To this day I am convinced that the reason it took me so long to get into the Pro Football Hall of Fame was because of the attention I received in New York. Let's face it, the sportswriters representing Green Bay didn't like me because I was always beating up on Jimmy Taylor and the sportswriters in Cleveland wouldn't vote for me because I was always going after Jimmy Brown.

I'll tell you something else. In 1959 I was named the NFL's defensive MVP. After "The Violent World of Sam Huff" aired in 1960, I didn't even make All Pro. I had a better year in 1960 than I did in 1959. Go figure.

Another reoccurring problem that I had to deal with was challenges from the general public. I would walk into a restaurant or bar and there would always be some wannabe badass who would feel it necessary to get in my face and challenge me.

This one time I was sitting at a bar, minding my own business when this guy came over and pulled up a stool next to me. He said, "You're Sam Huff, aren't you? Well, you don't look so tough to me. I think I can take you."

By now I'd had it. I got right into his face and said, "You might be able to take me, but I'll tell you this, you better make a commitment, because if you can't take me out, you're a dead man. I'll kill you. I'll take your head right off your shoulders."

With that he backed off.

"I was just kidding," he said.

"Well, I'm not. You want to challenge me? You're on, asshole!"

That guy was out of there like a shot.

On the other hand, I received a great compliment from Artie Donovan, the former Baltimore Colt tackle and Hall of Fame member. We were in Baltimore some years back and he said to me, "Sam, every defensive player who ever played this game owes you a debt of gratitude."

That was as good a reward as any.

1960: Jim Lee's Final Season

The 1960 season began with a bang. We won our first three games—all on the road—against San Francisco, St. Louis and Pittsburgh. Player injuries began to mount up. Alex Webster had a severe knee injury and ended up missing most of the season, Charlie Conerly had a minor elbow injury, but was able to return to action in week six against Cleveland. We beat the Browns 17–13 and held Jimmy Brown and his offense to six yards net on the ground which included 29 yards in 11 carries for Brown.

Early in the game, Little Mo's hand was stepped on by a cleat from an opposing player, which practically severed two of his fingers. The gash was extremely deep and blood was gushing all over. Mo held up his hand and started screaming at me to call time out.

No way! I wasn't about to waste a timeout on an injury. We only had three timeouts a half, and besides, we were coached not to call timeout on defense because the offense would need those valuable timeouts during the final two minutes.

I went over to Mo and grabbed both his fingers tight to help stop the bleeding.

"I'm not calling time out, Mo. We're gonna stop 'em right here and we'll get you out of here."

He looked at me as if I'd lost my mind. Mo glared at me, shook his head and said, "Man, I've seen some cold-blooded people in this game, but you are the worst!"

He pulled his hand away, made his way back to the line, and continued to play the next few downs. We ended up stopping the Browns and the offense came on to the field.

Mo ended up getting eight stitches and I wouldn't be surprised if he hasn't forgiven me to this day.

The following week we went on to beat the Steelers 27–24. Going into Week 8 we held on to a 5–1–1 record with the Eagles up next, but there was a slight problem. Due to an oversight in scheduling, we were forced to face Philly in back-to-back games in which the first would be played in Yankee Stadium and the second in Franklin Field.

To this day I always think about Frank Gifford when I reminisce about playing the Eagles. And each time I see Frank, it amazes me that he's not dead.

The talent that Philadelphia possessed was incredible. They had players such as Chuck Bednarik, Norm Van Brocklin, Tommy McDonald, and Pete Retzlaff. I always thought that we were better overall, but that season there was just something special about the Eagles.

The first game was played at Yankee Stadium. By the second quarter we had taken the lead 10–0. In the third quarter, Tommy McDonald scored making the score 10–7, and in the fourth, Bobby Walston kicked a field goal to tie. We ended up fumbling the ball, and the Eagles' Jimmy Carr ran 38 yards for the score. We were now down by seven with only minutes remaining in the game.

We were on the Eagle 30-yard line and driving when Frank took one of the most devastating hits I have ever seen on a football field.

George Shaw was quarterbacking and had Frank circle out of the back-field and across the middle. Unfortunately, he ran right in front of the Eagle's veteran middle linebacker Chuck Bednarik, the last of the two-way players. Bednarik was one of the toughest guys you ever saw. At 35 years of age and a 12-year veteran of the game, Chuck had decided to play one more season because he sensed the Eagles might make a run at the championship.

In my opinion, Frank shouldn't have been running that route. He tried to come underneath the linebackers—something that should always be avoided—especially against a seasoned vet like Bednarik. Chuck was one of those guys who would close in on you from behind and try to kill you.

That's exactly what he did to Gifford. Frank caught the ball and tried to get across the field when Bednarik just clotheslined him. He was hit so hard that he did a complete flip in the air and landed on the back of his head on the infield dirt. Not only was Frank knocked out, but he had fumbled the ball and the Eagles recovered.

Gifford lay motionless as Bednarik stood over him pounding his fist into his hand and jumping up and down celebrating the fumble recovery.

As our defense came on to the field, there was dead silence in the stands. I walked by Frank as he lay there on the ground, his face white and his body trembling from the shock of the hit as the medical staff worked on him. They took him out on a stretcher. As I entered the huddle, everyone was saying that it was all over for Gifford. There was no way he could survive a hit like that.

We were all visibly bothered by what had happened, but we managed to finish the game. We ended up losing 17–10, but that wasn't our main concern. As we entered the locker room, the medical staff was wheeling out a body covered with a sheet. One of the players yelled out, "Oh my God, it's Frank!"

We soon found out that it was the body of one of the security guards who had suffered a heart attack during the game.

That hit really took its toll on Gifford. He suffered a horrible concussion that put him in the hospital the rest of the week, sidelined him the rest of the year, and forced him to sit out the entire '61 season.

Bednarik was chastised for celebrating the controversial hit and took a lot of heat from the press and other players for doing so. On the other hand,

Frank never blamed Chuck for what he did. Gifford told a sportswriter, "He was just doing his job. I ran into him later and we sat down and had a beer. The thing never came up. We talked about his kids."

I never believed that Chuck meant for that to happen. It was in the the heat of the moment and his emotions took over. It was the greatest hit I'd ever seen—I'm only sorry *I* didn't get that hit. As a linebacker, you lie awake at night fantasizing about hits like that.

In the game of professional football people get hurt. It's part of the business and comes with the territory. Whenever you have contact you have violence. For example look at what happened between Raiders defensive back Jack Tatum and the Patriots' wide receiver Darryl Stingley.

Stingley was a star wide receiver with New England when he collided with Oakland defensive back Tatum on August 12, 1978. With one jolt, his life was forever changed. His neck was broken and he was left a quadriplegic. It was a terrible tragedy, but anyone who plays the game knows the risks involved.

Both Bednarik and Tatum were doing their jobs, and that makes what happened even harder to deal with.

The following week we played the Eagles again but this time at Franklin Field. Like the week prior, we came out smokin', scoring 17 points in the first quarter and holding Philly scoreless. Kyle Rote scored two TDs while Pat Summerall kicked a 35-yard field goal. With the exception of 31-yard field goal by Summerall, the second quarter belonged to the Eagles as they scored 17 points making the score at the half 20–17, Giants. Summerall kicked another field goal in the third, but the Eagles came roaring back with two TD passes from Norm Van Brocklin to Ted Dean and Billy Ray Barnes. Final score: Eagles 31, Giants 23.

To add insult to injury, the expansion Cowboys tied us 31–31 at home after losing 10 straight games. We beat the Redskins in Washington 17–3, but lost to the Cleveland Browns 48–34 in Jim Lee Howell's final game of his coaching career.

We ended the season with a 6–4–2 record. The Howell era produced three conference titles and a world championship.

1961: The Torch Is Passed—Head Coach Allie Sherman

Allie Sherman took over for Jim Lee Howell at the beginning of the 1961 season. To this day I despise the man, but back then as long as he left our defense alone, I could tolerate him.

In actuality Sherman was an excellent offensive coach and a great student of the game. His ideas were good, his game plans interesting, and he was one of the first people to put men in motion. He also had a good eye for offensive talent. But best of all, he also had absolutely nothing to do with our defense.

My old linebacker teammate Harland Svare was now an assistant coach assigned to the defense, but in reality, the defense coached itself. Sherman literally stayed away from us. He never attended meetings with us or even spoke to us…which was more than fine with me. We were still following Landry's defenses—which worked just fine, and besides, Sherman was far more interested in overhauling his offense.

Our offensive unit had now grown old and lacked in speed. Our quarterback Charlie Conerly was almost 40 and Gifford was advised by his doctors not to return to football.

That year training camp was held at Fairfield University in Connecticut. Everyone sensed that something was in the works—and it was. Soon after camp started, Wellington Mara came to one of our defensive meetings and asked us what we thought of the San Francisco 49er veteran quarterback Y.A. Tittle.

Wellington told us that the Giants may be acquiring him, and wanted to get some feedback from the guys who had played against him on defense. We all agreed that Y.A. would be an asset to the team. Tittle had been around for 12 years and was one of the best in the game. He could drive defenses mad, had an excellent feel for the game, ran the bootleg with the best of them, and was a terrific screen passer.

49ers coach Red Hickey wanted to bring in the shotgun offense and wanted to take advantage of his three younger quarterbacks who could run. They were Billy Kilmer, Bobby Waters, and John Brodie. Kilmer was a triple threat because he could pass, receive, and was a hell of a runner. The shotgun was not designed for an aging quarterback like Y.A. who was 34 at the time, so he became expendable.

When we finished camp and left for our West Coast exhibition games, the trade was not yet official. We ended up playing the 49ers in Portland, Oregon, and were told that if Y.A. got into the game that we were not to hurt him in any way.

The 49ers opened up the game with the shotgun. I thought that it was a dumb offense to use all the time. We stopped them cold and were winning in the fourth quarter when they put in Y.A. All of a sudden we could no longer rush the quarterback, and hitting him was out of the question. Tittle almost pulled out the win for the 'Niners.

The Acquisition of Y.A. Tittle

After the game the 49ers informed Tittle that he had been traded to New York for offensive guard and first-round draft choice Lou Cordileone. It turned out to be one of the greatest trades of all time.

But right off the bat there was a quarterback controversy. We still had Conerly, who reluctantly came back for one final year, as well as Don Heinrich and Lee Grosscup on the roster. Y.A.'s offensive teammates didn't exactly make him feel at home, therefore, he began to hang around with the defense. We were all veterans of the game and he knew we appreciated him.

Tittle loved to play cards. He introduced us to an old Louisiana card game called Boo Ray. The rules were really complicated and Y.A. was always winning. We called him the Boo Ray King. The most any one of us would lose was a few dollars a day and Y.A. was right in the middle of the action.

Even with our support, Tittle had some reservations about the team. In San Francisco he had the offensive talent of the Million Dollar Backfield, which consisted of Joe Perry, Hugh McElhenny, and John Henry Johnson, not to mention the talents of Billy Wilson and R.C. Owens. In New York he had flanker Kyle Rote who had a bad knee and fullback Alex Webster, who was all banged up.

One night Y.A. and I went out to dinner and while we were sitting there he kept shaking his head and saying, "We can't win here."

"What are you talking about?" I asked him

"Well, Kyle can't run anymore, Gifford is out, Webster's beat up, I got Phil King in the backfield and he's slow. We've got no speed whatsoever."

I looked him dead in the eye and said, "Let me tell you something, Yat. We win here. It's great to have you because you're going to score a lot of points for us. But we can win with you or without you; it won't make any difference to us because this team wins with defense, always has and always will, and don't ever forget it. All you need to do is get us ahead by three, and we'll take care of the rest."

Later on Y.A. told me that he appreciated what I'd said to him. We developed a great friendship and respected each other immensely. He used to always kid me about a late hit that I put on him when he was with San Francisco. I sacked him and he ended up at the bottom of the pile. As I was lying there I felt someone pinching my stomach. It was Tittle. He was pissed off about getting sacked so he pinched me in retaliation. His competitive spirit always showed through.

A few days after Y.A. had voiced his concerns regarding his offensive unit, the Giants made some great trades. One of those trades had to do with the Los Angeles Rams. Giants public relations director Don Smith met with Rams general manager Elroy Hirsch. The Rams wanted desperately to draft Roman Gabriel, a 6'5" quarterback out of North Carolina State as their first pick in the 1962 draft, but the Giants held the second pick.

Hirsch began to throw out a couple of names that the Rams were considering trading. One of those names was end Del Shofner. Y.A. played in a Pro Bowl game with Del and told Wellington that he thought he was one of the best receivers in the league, and requested that he make the trade for him. The following week, Shofner became a Giant, the Rams acquired Roman Gabriel the following year, and Y.A. never again complained about his offensive unit.

Every night before a home game, Tittle, Shofner, Don Chandler, Joe Morrison, and I would all go out to dinner. We always flipped a coin to see who would pay. Tittle was extremely farsighted—not to mention extremely vain—and refused to wear his glasses in public, therefore, he usually lost the coin flip. What the hell, quarterbacks made more than everyone else. He could afford the bill.

The Giants continued to draft good players. We acquired a tight end from the Redskins by the name of Joe Walton. He had good hands and was a devastating blocker. Joe ended up becoming an outstanding offensive coordinator under George Allen and later was named head coach of the New York Jets. The addition of Shofner allowed Sherman to permanently place Kyle Rote at the flanker position. Mel Triplett was traded to the Vikings, and Webster worked his ass off to get in shape to play the fullback position.

As far as the defense was concerned, we got defensive back Erich Barnes from the Bears. He was a great help to our secondary. Now, with all the characters in position, the 1961 New York Giants were ready to take on the NFL.

But then, the unexpected happened…

In a preseason game against the Rams, Tittle got hurt on his first play as a Giant. On a bobbled center exchange, Y.A. fell on the ball and two Rams fell on top of him. He ended up with two fractured vertebrae in his back and on injured reserve for a period of five weeks.

When the regular season began, Tittle was just about ready to play, but Sherman thought it would be better to go with Conerly. After all, he had played throughout the preseason.

Our first regular-season game was against the Cardinals at home. Charlie had a really bad day with only nine completions for 75 yards. There were three turnovers that led to three St. Louis touchdowns. Final score: St. Louis 21, New York 10.

Conerly started against the Steelers in game two. When Charlie had trouble getting the job done, Sherman sent in Y.A. And Tittle shined. He completed his first eight passes as a Giant and finished 10 of 12 for 123 yards. Shofner caught seven passes, and Webster ran for 82 yards. Final score: Giants 17, Steelers 14.

Week 3 saw us at Washington against the Redskins. Sherman decided to give Charlie one more try. Conerly threw an interception in the first quarter and Allie didn't hesitate to bring in Y.A. Charlie was furious about being pulled out, and he let Allie know it.

Nonetheless, Tittle ended up completing 24 passes for 315 yards. We beat Washington 24–21, and Y.A. became the new field general. He marched the team to a victory against the Cardinals and Cowboys, but when we played against the Rams in Week 6, Y.A. began to struggle.

When the Rams opened up a 14–10 lead in the third quarter, Sherman put Conerly back in. Charlie threw a TD pass to Kyle Rote, which put the Giants up 17–14, then threw 37 yards to Del Shofner for another score. We beat Los Angeles 24–14 and held on to a 5–1 record.

Conerly may have been the hero of the Ram game, but Y.A. was slated to start against Dallas. We lost 17–16.

Week 8 saw us at home against the Redskins once again. Y.A.'s arm was in pain all week. He hardly practiced, and at our pregame meal he told me, "Sam, I don't know what you're going to do today because I don't think I can play. My arm is killing me. I haven't practiced all week. I haven't even thrown a ball."

Just then he showed me his arm. He could hardly lift it. It was literally covered in black and blue bruises, and kickoff was in four hours. Nevertheless, Y.A. still started the game, and what a game he had. To this day I don't know how he did it. He completed 15 of 28 passes and threw for three touchdowns. We not only annihilated Washington, but shut them out 53–0.

The following week our locker room attendant, Pete Previte, came up with a play that caught everyone off guard. I know what you're thinking. The locker room attendant?

Pete worked the same job for the Yankees, and even though baseball and football are two completely different games, he came up with an interesting idea. When a baseball team needs speed, it puts in a pinch-runner. Why not do the same in football? Pete went to the blackboard and began diagramming the play.

The only speed we had on offense was Shofner. What if we included Erich Barnes and Jimmy Patton with the offense? Here's how the three of them would set up. We wanted to send all of them, plus a flanker and a running back, out in patterns as well.

No one gave Pete's idea much thought. No one, that is, except Allie Sherman. He implemented the play in the first half of the Eagles game. The ball was on our 38-yard line when Patton and Barnes were brought in. When they lined up on opposite sides, the Eagles were completely lost. They didn't know what to do. They had their linebacker Maxie Baughan covering Barnes and he just blew him away. Jetting down the field on a fly pattern and Y.A. coming out of the shotgun, they connected for a 62-yard touchdown. The play was put into the books and was named the Pete Previte Special.

Tittle threw for three touchdowns that day, and we beat Philly 38–21. Our record was now 7–2. With four regular-season games left to play, we began looking toward another division championship. With wins over Pittsburgh, Cleveland, and Philly (again) and only one loss to Green Bay, all we had to do was tie the Browns for the crown. And that's exactly what we did.

We tied Cleveland with a score of 7–7. Sherman won Coach of the Year, Tittle won MVP, Shofner set a new club record with 68 receptions for 11 touchdowns, and Webster finished the regular season with 928 yards rushing—the third best in the league.

Once again we would get a shot at the championship, but we knew it wouldn't be easy. We would be playing the Packers in ice-cold Green Bay. The day we arrived the temperature was five below zero, and the Packer fans were there in full force to meet us. 5,000 screaming fans booed us as we stepped off the tarmac.

I never really liked Green Bay, and they, in turn, didn't exactly welcome me with open arms. The rivalry between Jimmy Taylor and me was infamous.

The day of the game, the field was frozen and the temperature was 15 degrees with 10- to 15-miles-per hour winds. The conditions were so bad that we practiced in tennis shoes. We wore our regular cleats during the game, but it really didn't matter what we wore. The Packers were ready for us.

Neither team scored in the first quarter, but from then on, it was all Green Bay. At the half it was 24–0 and Y.A. had four of his passes intercepted. Tittle was 6-for-20, and Sherman sent in Conerly. That didn't change anything.

Paul Hornung and Taylor gained 158 yards rushing while the Pack held us to only 31. Alex Webster sprained his ankle in the first half and was out of the game. Hornung set a record by scoring 19 points—a touchdown, three field goals, and four extra points.

Due to all the injuries on the team, our running back Joe Morrison had to play on defense at safety. He had to cover the Packers tight end Ron Kramer. Morrison didn't have a chance.

In the end, it was another bitter loss for the Giants in a championship game. We were shut out 37–0.

Nemesis: Sherman and Taylor

Following the end of the '61 season, Mary and I decided to make New York our permanent place of residence. Our children were older now and the educational opportunities were better here in the big city. I also began to think of my life after football, and the opportunities for employment were far greater in New York than in West Virginia.

In the off-season I was still employed by Philip Morris. I was hoping to work full-time for the company, you know, looking toward the future after my playing days were over. But they were content with me working part-time, giving speeches and making appearances.

One day I received a call to give a speech (for a separate company) in Memphis. I was offered $500 and all expenses paid. I accepted and took off for Memphis. I gave my speech to a receptive audience. In that audience was a sales rep from Philip Morris. He called the marketing executive in New York and told him what I had done.

The following Monday I was called into his office. He was livid. Little did I know that I had unknowingly violated my contract with Philip Morris. He said, "You're not supposed to be doing things like that. We're paying you to work for us and on your day off you're charging people for a speech. That's like stealing as far as I'm concerned!"

When he accused me of stealing, I went ballistic. "Stealing? On my own time? On my day off? Don't you ever accuse me of stealing you son of a bitch! I work five days a week for the company, 10 to 12 hours a day, and the way I spend my day off is nobody's business but my own!"

I took my company credit card out of my pocket and threw it in his face. I was so pissed that I was ready to throw this guy out the window. All of a sudden my friend, Jack Landry, came running into the room and got between us. Jack got me out of the room and calmed me down. I told him I was quitting. Appearances had already been scheduled for me for the next three months. Because of my friendship with Jack, I agreed to honor the commitment. But my relationship and employment with the Philip Morris Company was now history.

It's always been said that when one door closes, another opens. And that's exactly what happened. During the '62 training camp some marketing people from J.P. Stevens, a huge textile company based in New York City, asked me if I would be interested in doing some commercials. I agreed.

After working for the company for a while, I inquired if there was any possibility of working for them year-round. They told me that they were looking for a spokesperson to work with customers when they came to New York. I was offered to try out the job for six months. If they liked me and I liked them, I would become a full-time employee.

Two months later I was told that I had the job for as long as I wanted it. I stayed with the J.P. Stevens for seven years and learned the all about sales and marketing within the textile business.

Of course, football was still my No. 1 priority. 1962 saw quite a few major changes in the ballclub. Conerly finally retired after 14 seasons, Kyle Rote's knees couldn't withstand another season, so he hung up his cleats, put on a whistle, and became Sherman's backfield coach. Pat Summerall had been working part-time in the broadcasting business and retired to become a full-time broadcaster. It was now up to Don Chandler to do the place-kicking and punting. Frank Gifford spent the last year in the broadcast booth, but decided to return to football once again as a player.

The new roster would look like this: With Rote retired, Gifford would be shifted to flanker, Joe Morrison, Phil King and Paul Dudley would alternate the halfback position and Webster would continue playing fullback. On defense, Cliff Livingston was traded to the Vikings and replaced with a rookie from St. Olaf College in Minnesota by the name of Bill Winter.

None of us knew it at the time, but if you were to study Sherman's draft history and major moves, you would see that his main concentration was in beefing up the offense. He continued to ignore the defense, and in the long run it would cost him dearly.

The '62 season also saw Andy Robustelli and Jimmy Patton as player-coaches for our defensive unit, which in reality, meant that we were once again coaching ourselves, which was okay with me. But during training camp, Sherman decided to scrap Landry's inside-outside 4-3 defense. He wanted me to go to the strong side gap—the side the tight end was on—to plug the hole between the center and the guard. If the play went to the other side, I would be caught in traffic and couldn't get through to make the play. Unless the play came directly at me, I was virtually useless.

The exhibition season proved that this defense wasn't gong to work, but Allie continued to go with it. I went to Andy and told him that I couldn't play this way all of the time. Andy said, "Sam, I agree with you, but this is the defense Allie wants you to play, and you're just going to have to do it."

His answer wasn't good enough, so I went to see Sherman. I went into his office and said, "Allie, can you please explain your philosophy on this defense because I can't play it all the time. I can't make tackles from sideline to sideline the way I'm used to doing. I'm just taking one gap and I can't go out in pursuit, and that's going to kill this football team."

Sherman's eyes narrowed. He looked at me and said, "You know, Sam, you're always bitching. Why don't you just play the defense the way it's designed? That's the way I want it and that's the way you'll play it. If you're going to play on this team, you're going to play my defense."

I told him I would, but walked out of his office shaking my head in disbelief. Luckily for us our offense was hot all season and scored an incredible number of points. Our defense gave up more points and yards, but between Y.A., Gifford, and Shofner, it didn't matter. Following a 3–2 start, we won our last nine games, which included a 49–34 victory over the Redskins. Tittle completed 27 of 39 throws in that game, including 12 consecutive passes. He threw for seven touchdowns which tied the league record.

After the game, Y.A. was being interviewed by the media and was asked why he didn't throw for an eighth touchdown pass. His answer was as classy as the man himself. "It would have been in bad taste. If you're leading by so much, it just doesn't sit right with me to fill the air with footballs. I'm the quarterback; it would be showing off."

That year our defense never had the chance to show off—at least not with that ridiculous system we were playing. We were playing the Cardinals one week, and they had a great running back by the name of John David Crow who was just running over us in the first half. Because we were still using Allie's ineffective defense, Crow was running through all the holes. Rosey Grier was getting blocked from all sides, and I couldn't get to the hole because I was going to the strong side and couldn't get back in time.

Halftime finally came, and we hit the locker room. I was furious, but knew I couldn't say anything. I had finally had enough, and when we got into our defensive huddle at the start of the second half, I glared at Robustelli and said, "Godammit, Andy! You're going to let that little son of a bitch Sherman ruin us! Well he's not going to ruin me! I've had it! We're getting murdered by Crow! Why don't you stand up to Sherman and tell him what we've got to do?"

Andy looked at me and said, "Okay, Sam. But let's play the inside-outside without telling anybody. We'll just do it and worry about the consequences later."

It was the first time I smiled all season.

The Cardinals were leading 14–10 at the half, but all that changed. We implemented that 4-3 defense and completely shut them down. When the final whistle blew, the Giants had come from behind to beat St. Louis 31–28.

When we reported to practice on Tuesday, Sherman was waiting for us, and he was steaming mad. He immediately began screaming at us, and the veins in his neck began to pop out. "Let me tell you something. When I put up a defense, you will play that defense. Do I make myself understood? And you will go back to playing that defense the way it is designed to be played! Do you understand?"

We reverted back to that stupid defense, but the offense made up for its weaknesses; that is, until we played the Packers for the championship. Once again we clinched the division and once again Sherman was voted Coach of the Year. Why, I'll never know.

The game was played at Yankee Stadium, but the weather was definitely Green Bay weather. The temperature was 20 degrees and dropping and the wind was blowing 35 miles per hour. For me personally, it was the worst weather I'd ever played in. It was so cold that a couple of the guys developed frostbite when the game was over.

The sensationalism that had built up before the game was always about Jimmy Taylor and me. We had that fierce rivalry, and Jimmy was always saying, "I love to sting people. I like to find people and just run over them."

To a linebacker, those are fightin' words and I was ready to face him in battle.

I never met a competitor like Taylor. He's still that way today. Whether it's a golf game or a tennis match, he will play like his life depended on it. On the field he would swear at you, kick you, gouge you, spit at you, whatever it took to intimidate you. He ran low and hard, and he'd kick you in the head with his knees. The one thing I liked about Taylor was that I didn't have to go far to find him. He would try to find you so he could run over you. He never took the easy route. And he was always shooting his mouth off. After you would hit him he'd say things like, "I only got four this time, but next time I'll get more."

I'd yell back, "Oh, yeah! Let's see you come in here and get it!"

His own teammates would tell him to shut up. They knew that the more he talked, the more pissed off the defense got. Jimmy was also a great option runner. He would get a handoff and head off tackle following his blocking, and he had the choice of going outside or cutting in. If he came inside he knew I would be there to meet him. On one memorable play in the '62 title game, Taylor decided to take it outside and I went with the flow. It was right in front of the Giants bench, and I can remember thinking to myself, "Okay, it's live or die right now."

I slammed into him with every ounce of energy and strength that I had. I don't remember getting up, but when I did regain my senses, I noticed that there was a major dent in my helmet from where his knee hit my head. That banged-up helmet now resides in the Pro Football Hall of Fame.

Throughout the entire game, Jimmy bitched every time he was hit. He even accused me of biting him. Now how could I bite him with a face mask on? The only way that could have happened was if his hand was inside of my face mask.

Y.A. didn't have a good day. The weather was a big factor, along with linebacker Ray Nitschke. Tittle completed only 18 of 41 passes. Every time he'd throw the ball the wind would knock it down. Plus, Nitschke was all over Y.A. and blitzing at will. At the end of the first half, the Packers were leading 10–0.

At the beginning of the third quarter, Erich Barnes blocked a Max McGee punt and our end, Jim Collier, recovered it in the end zone for a touchdown. That would be the only score the Giants would make all day. Jerry Kramer kicked two more field goals, and once again the Packers won by a score of 16–7.

I was already upset about losing the game; then I heard Taylor mouthing off to the press. "Sam Huff was hitting me with cheap shots as well as biting and piling on. The man is the dirtiest player in the league. He tried to cripple me. He used his elbows and his knees when I was on the ground.

"I was just beginning to get up when somebody piled on me and I bit my tongue. I was spitting blood for the rest of the game. I think Huff hit me with his elbow in the first period. Sam Huff is a great one for piling on. He always has done it. Sam likes being there on top of the pile. Somebody was in there twisting my head, and someone was in there digging a shoulder or an elbow into me. I had a few words with Huff about it."

Jimmy was entitled to his opinion, and I wasn't about to deny that my main objective was to knock him down hard. But in those days, and in the minds of the players, this was not considered dirty football. This was also a world championship game and the Giants were not about to be humiliated a second time.

Another thing that really bothered me was that Sherman never defended me or backed me up. I took great pride in my style of play, and Allie never once said anything positive about me. I decided to take matters into my own hands.

I got a group of sportswriters together to view the game films. I let them decide whether or not I was a dirty player. Whatever the consensus, it would be written the following day in their column. But something strange happened. After reviewing the film, they all felt that Nitschke was the dirtiest guy on the field—not me. They all ended up defending me.

When the game had ended, Taylor checked himself into the hospital. I should have done the same. I had a severe concussion.

A few weeks following the game, I received a picture in the mail. It showed the referee setting the football down long after the whistle had blown, and me holding Taylor in a headlock.

Like I said before, it was a different game back then.

THIRD QUARTER
TRADED!

Ego vs. Football Logic

Forty-six years have passed since that jerk Allie Sherman traded me to the Washington Redskins, and to this day I still haven't forgiven him for what he did.

I have no doubt that Sherman deliberately set out to destroy the Giants' defensive unit. I also believe that his arrogance and over-inflated ego superseded football logic. Landry's defense was built around the unit's individual talents, and was adjusted to meet opponents' offenses or new personnel. But since it wasn't a defense that Allie created, he methodically and systematically devised a way to destroy it

The first indication of his plan was the trade of Cliff Livingston in 1962. After Cliff's departure, I ended my final two seasons as a Giant playing with three different strongside linebackers. In '62 rookie Bill Winter replaced Livingston and played the position until he became injured that same year. He was replaced by Jerry Hillebrand, our top draft pick in 1962. Even though Jerry was an All-American out of Colorado he was drafted as a tight end and spent the '62 season on the taxi squad learning how to play the linebacker position.

Sherman also refused to use high draft choices on outstanding college players for the defensive team. One of his biggest blows to the defensive unit was the 1963 trade of Rosey Grier to the Rams in exchange for John LoVetere.

Rosey ended up having some pretty good years with the Rams, while LoVetere blew out a knee in '64 and was forced to quit the game.

Other changes included the trade of our veteran center Ray Wietecha, who was replaced by Greg Larson.

The '63 Season

We began the season with a 37–28 victory over the Baltimore Colts. Y.A. was having a great day and had thrown for three touchdowns, but late in the game he was hit so hard that he had to be taken off the field.

It was obvious that Tittle was too banged up to play the following week, so his backup, Ralph Guglielmi, was slated to start against Pittsburgh.

In the locker room that Sunday, Allie Sherman gave this speech to his team. "We will probably lose this game today, but I'm not going to risk the whole season by playing Y.A. We'll just go out there and play without him."

Have you ever heard a head coach announce to his team that they didn't have a chance to win the game? What an asshole! We ended up getting shut out 31–0!

After the game, Sherman stormed into the locker room. He was absolutely furious and tried to rip out the wires for the postgame radio show. He was literally swinging from the cables! He blamed Ralph Guglielmi for the loss and immediately traded him to Philadelphia. Here Ralph is on his way to Philly and we're scheduled to play the Eagles the following week. I would be lying if I said we weren't a little concerned about what we were going to do if Ralph got in the game. With the Redskins' starter Sonny Jurgensen injured, there was a good chance that this would happen.

The day of the game had King Hill starting in place of Jurgensen. Early in the game we blitzed the Philly offense and I hit King with a clean shot and knocked him out of the game. So in comes Ralph.

On the first play, Robustelli charged through the line and hit Ralph, breaking three of his ribs. The only person left who could play the quarterback position was Jurgensen. He was really hurting, and the Giants intercepted four of his passes. We ended up beating them 37–14.

That year Jerry Hillebrand played on my left side and a guy by the name of Tom Scott was on my right. Scott was one of those players with raw talent, and he had a mean streak like you wouldn't believe. He would just beat guys up. He was known for wearing a large hockey pad on his elbow, which he used to clobber people. His pregame warmup was beating on his locker. He had a wild look on his face and you could swear he was frothing at the mouth. During the Browns game he got into a fight with Jim Brown, and both of them were thrown out of the game.

In Week 5 we played Cleveland at home and went into the game with a 3–1 record. We ended up losing 35–24. The following week we were victorious over the Cowboys, and in Week 7 we played the Browns in Cleveland. Once again we shut down Jim Brown, holding him to 40 yards on nine carries, beating Cleveland 33–6. We continued our win streak by beating the Cardinals, the Eagles, and the 49ers.

Sunday, November 24 we were scheduled to play the Cardinals at home. President John F. Kennedy had been assassinated in Dallas, Texas just two days previous, on Friday, November 22, 1963. Like the rest of the world, we were in shock. I had gotten to be friends with President Kennedy and even campaigned for him in West Virginia in 1960. What was even more shocking was that Commissioner Pete Rozelle had decided that all NFL games would be played as scheduled. The games should have been cancelled—hell, nobody was thinking about football at a time like that.

We played the Cardinals as scheduled and I can't remember one thing about that game other than we lost, but that seemed totally insignificant at the time. Neither the Giants nor the Cardinals had their mind on the game, and it was probably the worst game of football I've ever played in.

Our final game of the season pitted us against the Steelers. This was a must-win game in order for us to play in the championship game.

We lit up the Steelers with a 16–0 lead, but Pittsburgh fired right back to make the score 16–10. In the second half Gifford broke the game wide open with a terrific one-handed catch on third-and-8 from deep in our own territory. Final score: Giants 33, Steelers 17. It was our third straight conference title and once again, Y.A. set an NFL record with 36 touchdown passes. He also had a 60 percent completion rate, a new team record. Shofner had 64 receptions and Gifford caught 42 passes, including seven touchdowns. Our offense scored 448 points in 14 games. We were awesome—until we faced the Chicago Bears in the championship game.

Under Coach George Allen, the Bears defense only allowed 144 points for the season. They used a double zone in the secondary, led the league in defending against the pass, and had the most interceptions—36. It would be the classic matchup: the best offense against the best defense. The Giants were 10 point favorites, even with the game being played at Wrigley Field.

Like years prior, the conditions were brutal. It was nine degrees at kickoff and the field was frozen solid. One of my main concerns was Chicago's tight end, Mike Ditka. After studying film on him, I noticed that he would stick out an elbow and cheap-shot you if he saw you standing around doing nothing.

I wasn't about to deal with Ditka's elbow, so before the game I told Jerry Hillebrand that we were going to make sure that Ditka got a special delivery message on the subject of unnecessary roughness. "Jerry, you get over Ditka's outside shoulder and when he comes off the ball, nail him right in the face mask and knock him back toward me in the middle and then I will knock him back toward you."

On the first series we hit Ditka hard. Mike started shouting, "What are you guys trying to do to me?"

I looked at him and said, "Mike, I've been watching the films, and I've seen what you've been doing to some people. I happen to play by the rules of the game, and that's how I'd like this game to be played. Why don't you try it?"

We never had another problem with Mike for the rest of the afternoon. He ended up catching only one pass all day, but that was the least of our problems.

After opening up the game with a 7–0 lead on a 14-yard pass from Tittle to Gifford, Del Shofner dropped a touchdown that was placed right in his hands. On the next play, Y.A.'s pass was intercepted by Larry Morris of the Bears and returned to the Giant 5. Two plays later Chicago quarterback Billy Wade ran the ball into the end zone to tie the game at seven all.

A little later in the game, the Giants had the opportunity to go up by a touchdown with second and goal at the Bears' 2-yard line. The offense wanted to bust a wedge play over the middle, but Allie Sherman insisted on calling a sweep. On second down, Joe Morrison was tackled for a loss as he tried to go left then was tackled again on third down on a sweep to the right. We ended up having to settle for a field goal and a 10–7 lead, which would come back to haunt us later on in the game.

In the second quarter Larry Morris blitzed and collided into Tittle's left knee. Y.A. was immediately sidelined and taken to the locker room as rookie Glynn Griffing replaced him.

At halftime, Tittle's knee was wrapped up. Even though he could barely walk on the leg, he was determined to play. I tried to talk him out of it. "Yat, stay out. We'll win it for you with the defense. Remember that conversation we had back in Portland when I told you all we needed was three? You got us the three, now let us get you that title. They can't move the ball on us. Just stay the hell out and we'll take care of it."

Tittle replied, "Sam, this is my last chance to win a championship. I've got to play. I want to wear that ring."

Y.A. hobbled on to the field, his knee completely wrapped in bandages. On the first play, Tittle limped back to throw a screen pass and Ed O'Bradovich intercepted it. He ran 10 yards downfield to the Giant 14. Five plays later, Wade called a quarterback sneak and the Bears were up 14–10. That's how the game ended.

The following day the papers gave their version of what had gone wrong and who was to blame. You didn't have to be a rocket scientist to know that if Tittle had been healthy, the Giants would have been the team wearing the rings.

But while I went off to work for J.P. Stevens, Allie Sherman was busy at work dismantling the team.

Traded to the Redskins!

The first to go was Dick Modzelewski, who was traded to the Browns in March. That really shocked me. A couple of days after the trade I went over to the Giants office to speak to Wellington Mara.

"What's going on, Wellington? Why in the world would you trade Mo?"

Wellington said, "Sam, I can't tell you everything because we're putting a lot of pieces together here and we think we have to make some changes."

I told him, "You've traded Livingston, you've traded Rosey, and now you've traded Mo. What about me? Am I next?"

Wellington looked me straight in the eye and said, "Nothing's going to happen to you, Sam. You don't ever have to worry. You're one of the family. We'll never trade you."

"Well," I said, "your word is good enough for me."

At that time he asked me to sign my contract for the '64 season. I was making somewhere around $17,000 a year and they were going to offer me $19,000. I told Wellington I wanted to think about it before signing.

"No problem," he said. "As long as you are here, why don't you stop and say hello to Allie before you leave."

To satisfy Wellington I walked down the hall to Allie's office. Although Sherman and I didn't see eye to eye, we tolerated each other. Throughout our differences, we were always able to communicate with each other.

I told Allie that I was a little concerned about him trading Mo to Cleveland and he said, "Don't worry about that, it's no problem."

With that, I left and didn't think much more about the issue.

A few weeks later, I had a sales meeting in Cleveland. While walking to my gate at the airport I ran into Don Smith. We talked briefly about Mo's trade. I jokingly said to Smitty that if the Giants ever traded me, I'd want to take him with me. We laughed and went to our respective gates.

That evening I had dinner at Ed Modzelewski's (Dick's older brother) restaurant in Cleveland. During the meal, a girl came over to the table and said there was phone call for him. Ed left the table and came back telling me that Mary had been looking for me.

She never did that, and the call really frightened me. I thought that maybe one of the kids had gotten hurt. I ran to the phone. "Mary, is everything okay?"

"Sam," she said, her voice quivering as if she had been crying. "Allie Sherman just called. You've been traded to the Washington Redskins."

I was in shock. I couldn't believe what I was hearing!

"Who did they get for me?"

"Halfback Dickie James and defensive end Andy Stynchula."

By this point I was completely stunned. Hell, just a few hours prior I'd spoke with Smitty, one of my best friends, and he didn't give any indication of me being traded. So I decided to call him, and ended up screaming into the phone, "Why didn't you tell me I was getting traded?"

"What are you talking about, Sam? The Giants would never trade you."

Don thought I was joking with him, but this was no joke. Those bastards at Giants' headquarters never even told Don Smith about the trade, and he was their PR person. Don said he would try to find out what was going on. He contacted Wellington and was told the truth. He was more upset than I was.

At the sale meeting I tearfully announced that I had played my last game in a Giants uniform. It was an extremely emotional time for me and I still get choked up whenever I talk about that day. I immediately got on the phone and called up Cleveland Browns owner Art Modell. I asked him if there was any way he could work out a deal with the Redskins that would get me to Cleveland. "Let me play for you, Art. I'd love to get a shot at the Giants."

"I'm sorry Sam, but there is nothing I can do."

I went home to Mary and the kids. When I arrived at the house in Flushing, there were reporters everywhere. They told me that the news of my trade to Washington had stopped the ticker tape on Wall Street. I had a stack of phone messages waiting for me and I returned every one of those calls that evening.

Later on that night I received a message to call Bob Stevens, the chairman of the board of J.P. Stevens. "You know, Sam, I've been reading about this trade in the newspaper and I just want you to know something. You've been with us for a while and you've been a great employee. I'll put this in writing if you want. I'll be your ace in the hole. If you want to go to the Redskins and continue to work for us, we'll work that out. If you don't want to play anymore, you have a job with us as long as you want it."

With the state I was in, I really appreciated his words and I needed that kind of support.

The following day I received a call from Wellington Mara. "I've got to talk to you, Sam. How about meeting me at the New York Athletic Club in an hour?"

"Fine, I'll be there."

It was all I could do to keep a civil tongue.

On the afternoon that we met, Wellington couldn't look me in the eye. As he talked to me, he stared out the window. "I don't know what to say. I lied to you."

I immediately struck back. "Yes, you did! You hurt me and you hurt me bad. You know, when I started playing for you we once argued over $500 on a contract. You got so mad you threw papers all over the room. You threatened me and you told me you would trade me so fast I wouldn't even know where I had landed. I signed the contract that day, and you gained my respect. But now, you will never have it again, because you lied to me!"

He never said a word, and I stormed out of the room.

Over the years Wellington and I settled our differences. I never believed that it was he who wanted to get rid of me. I knew it was Allie Sherman's call to make the trade. But in 1964, that was little consolation for me.

There I was, 29 years old and playing middle linebacker for one of the greatest teams in the league. And with one phone call, I was gone—traded by a coach whose personal ego superseded sound football judgment. Ever since he traded me, Sherman always told people I was slipping, that I was slowing down, that he'd talked to me about adjusting my game to his system but that I had refused. The defense was getting old and it was up to him to do something about it. Too old? Bullshit! I not only played five more years in the league, but I remained long enough to get my revenge on that bastard.

It also bothers me that Sherman never had the balls to call me into his office and tell me face to face about the trade. As far as I'm concerned, he can burn in hell. He single-handedly destroyed a great football team and in the process of doing so, hurt the careers and personal lives of many great people.

On one occasion, Sherman himself came very close to being destroyed by me.

A few weeks after the trade, I received a call from Jack Mara, Wellington's brother. He's always been a very nice man and dear friend. He asked me to play in the Giants' annual golf tournament in Westchester. To him I would always be a member of the Giants family and it would mean a lot to me if I could join my old teammates. He also had one other favor to ask. "Sam, I don't want a confrontation with Allie Sherman."

I told him, "I'll be there and I promise to avoid Sherman."

The latter didn't go as planned. After the round ended I went into the locker room to take a shower. As I was drying off, I saw Allie walking toward me. He came right up to me and said, "Maybe you think I need to explain to you why I traded you. Well, I don't think so."

"Get away from me, Sherman," I said. "I gave Jack Mara my word that I would avoid confrontation with you, or you'd be a dead man right now."

Just then Alex Webster and another golfer got between us. Alex escorted Allie from the scene. It's a good thing he did because the confrontation could have escalated into a brawl. But I'll tell you one thing, if I hadn't given Jack Mara my word, Sherman would not be alive today.

Years later, Wellington talked about the breakup of our football team in a book by Gerald Eskenazi titled, *There Were Giants in Those Days.*

> "It's easy now to look back. Allie believed the team was never going to be good enough to win the whole championship. He said we'd never be better than second best. I think he felt that maybe they were jaded or had gone as far as they were going to go.
>
> "Obviously I did agree with the trades after 1963 because I could have stopped any of those deals. But I didn't sense the era was ending."

By the time I'd been traded, the greatest era in the history of the New York Giants had ended. The '64 season ended with a catastrophic 2–10–2 record; in 1965, they were 7–7; in 1966, 1–12–1; in 1967, 7–7; and again in 1968, 7–7; including four straight losses at the end of the season that saw the demise of coach Allie Sherman.

To this day the bastard still lies to the media when asked about the trade. He once gave an interview and had this to say about what happened: "After that season, we reevaluated our ballclub. It was no longer a young team, and we felt we had to rebuild. Now Sam never laid down on us, but we felt we weren't going to get enough from him. It was a football decision, and that's all I really want to say about it. I didn't know Wellington said that Huff would not be traded. I talked over all my moves with management. I really don't want to get into a debate about it. I'll pick my own venue. I'm not going to go pro and con with you."

Now if you can figure out what he just said, would you please let me know. I don't have a clue as to what he was talking about. All I know is that the trade should have never happened. I knew it, the fans of New York knew it, Wellington Mara knew it, and Allie Sherman knew it.

That is why to this day I will never, ever forgive him for what he did to me.

Coach Bill McPeak and Attorney Edward Bennett Williams

When I finally accepted the fact that I would be playing for Washington, I decided that I would make the Redskins pay for my services. Even though I was still extremely passionate about the game, I realized that it was a business first and a game second. I was no longer that country boy from West Virginia. I'd been in New York for eight years and knew what I wanted, and the Redskins were going to have to meet my demands.

Coach Bill McPeak was my first contact with the Redskins. A week after the trade, he came to our house in Flushing to discuss game plans. Nothing was ever discussed about my contract.

McPeak was all football and had a great eye for talent. In 1963 he became general manager of the team and was given carte blanche to make improvement decisions regarding the team. He had already traded with the Eagles for Sonny Jurgensen. He needed a strong team leader who could run the offense, and Sonny was his man. He told me that his defensive unit would be built around me. McPeak was redesigning the entire team with Jurgensen and me as the nucleuses.

We met several more times before the question of salary arose. "How much will it take, Sam?" Bill said.

There was no hesitation in my answer. "If I'd stayed in New York I would have been making somewhere around $19,000. I won't come to Washington for anything les than $35,000."

Even with carte blanche, McPeak wasn't able to authorize that kind of salary, so he suggested that I talk to Edward Bennett Williams. Williams was the famous Washington attorney who had taken over the team from George Preston Marshall's family.

I flew to Washington to meet with Williams and was extremely intimidated by him. He represented people like Jimmy Hoffa, the Andrews Sisters,

1964, Sam and Sonny at Sam's first training camp with the Redskins after being traded by Allie Sherman and the Giants.

Sam as a Redskin. (AP)

Saigon, February 15, 1966. Johnny Unitas watches as NFL greats Willie Davis, Sam Huff, and Frank Gifford leap from a 1st infantry division tank during their visit with U.S. troops. (AP)

Sam sits in front of his locker after announcing his retirement from the NFL on December 12, 1967. (AP)

Player/coach Sam Huff stands with the legendary Vince Lombardi.

Sam manning the middle in his final year, 1969. (Getty)

Sam Huff, 1982 Hall of Fame inductee.

Linebacker

SAM HUFF

PRO
FOOTBALL
HALL
OF FAME

Hall of Famer Sam Huff with the Redskins.

Sam Huff (second from left) at Yankee Stadium with No. 81 Andy Robustelli, No. 16 Frank Gifford, No. 79 Rosie Brown, Tom Landry (far right), and longtime Giants owner Wellington Mara.

Sam and Sonny.

and many other big-time celebrities. It was the mid-'60s and agents and lawyers had not yet become an integral part of the game.

When I entered his office, the man immediately put me at ease. He told me how much the team wanted and needed me and that I would continue to wear No. 70—which was very important to me. He also said that the team would continue acquiring good players in order to make the Redskins a contender.

Now came the response to the request for $35,000. "You know Sam, that's a lot of money and that's a lot more than we pay any of our linebackers. It would be virtually unfair to pay any one guy twice as much as any of the other players are receiving. It's the principle of it all."

When I heard that, I went off. "Screw principle. I've been hearing that same damned principle crap from Wellington Mara for eight years now, so don't talk to me about principle. It doesn't mean a thing to me because the same guy who told me he wasn't ever going to trade me just traded me to you. How's that for principle?

"Mr. Williams, if you want me to play for the Redskins it is going to cost you $35,000, and not one penny less."

Williams knew that I meant business and replied, "Sam, I understand your position, so here's what we'll do. I'll give you a $30,000 player contract and we'll write it in that for another $5,000, you'll also do some scouting for us in the off-season. Bottom line, it's $35,000."

I told him we had a deal.

Carlisle, Pennsylvania—Training Camp

Training camp was located in Carlisle, Pennsylvania. I promised myself that I would attend camp and not make trouble. I was the new guy there, and had played against many of the Washington players. Now I had to come in and make friends with people I'd been competing against and didn't particularly like. I'm sure they felt the same about me. Look at it this way, I had played on the Giants '61 team that had beaten the Redskins 53–0. In fact, the Giants held a 12-game unbeaten streak over the Redskins going all the way back to 1957, and I played in every one of those games.

I thought it would be best that I didn't drive to camp. In New York, no one had a car, but when I arrived at Carlisle, I counted seven Cadillacs in the players' parking lot. Not only were they driving expensive cars, but each dorm room had a refrigerator stocked with beer. It was more like a country club than a training camp. The Redskins would pay for the players' laundry and dry cleaning, there were maids to clean up your room, locker room attendants to sweep up after you, and college kids to take away your food trays at the cafeteria.

The Giants players were more considerate of others. They took up collections for the maids and the college kids who served us food in the dorms. The Redskins didn't do that, not until I began the tradition that summer. I also helped set up an executive players committee and of course, McPeak wanted me to help install Landry's 4-3 defense. That was the only defense we practiced in training camp.

The Redskins were never known as a disciplined team, which made the players an interesting group of guys. Everything was disorganized, not to mention dysfunctional. The team's founder, George Preston Marshall, was as tight as they come, and ran the club in the same manner.

The front office was totally disorganized and virtually nonexistent. Their PR man, Dave Slattery, was negotiating player contracts and there was no receiver coach for the team. Future Hall of Famer Bobby Mitchell never had a receiver coach working with him on pass patterns. He pretty much coached himself and ran whatever routes he and the quarterbacks would came up with.

Another Colorful Cast of Characters

Former Colts cornerback Johnny Sample was on the roster. He was a gambler, drove the coaches crazy, and was brazen when it came to the rules. For example, there was a circular drive in front of our dorm and McPeak made it clear that the players were not to park their cars there. It was for the coaching staff only. He no sooner gave the order than Johnny's car, a big, green Cadillac, was parked in the driveway right next to the front door.

We had a defensive end by the name of John Paluck. We nicknamed him Mean John. He was an inch away from being certifiably insane. He was a real tough player. As a matter of fact, he's one of the few guys I played with who literally scared me. No one ever messed with him.

In addition to Sonny and me, McPeak made quite a few trades that year. We acquired a receiver from the Bears by the name of Angelo Coia and defensive tackle Fred Williams, who we called Fat Fred. Baltimore sent us kicker Jim Martin and fullback J.W. Lockett and the Steelers gave up receiver Preston Carpenter and linebacker John Reger. Philadelphia gave up defensive back Jim Carr and the Browns traded away defensive back Jim Shorter.

The draft picks weren't too bad either. McPeak and our chief scout, Bucko Kilroy, took Arizona running back and future Hall of Famer Charley Taylor as their first pick. Charley didn't move to the split end position until Otto Graham became coach in 1966. They also drafted future All-Pro center Len Hauss out of Georgia and another future Hall of Famer, defensive back Paul Krause of Iowa. McPeak had a terrific eye for talent. Jurgensen also utilized flanker Bobby Mitchell, a future Hall of Fame member who became the first black player in the history of the Redskin franchise.

Even with the talent that McPeak and Kilroy had obtained, our offense was still pretty bad. The offensive line was one of the worst I'd ever seen, and Sonny was lucky to have escaped with his life that season. I can't say much different for our defense. The unit was totally undisciplined, not to mention ragged. There was no rhyme or reason to the current system so we implemented the 4-3. My former Giant teammate Ed Hughes was our defensive coach. Ed and I never saw eye to eye when we were in New York, and the friction between us grew worse in Washington.

One time we got beat when a tight end came over the middle and caught a deep pass late in the game. I had taken my key and stayed with the running back while the player behind me blew his coverage. Ed blamed me for the missed coverage and told the press the same. Without hesitation I let him have it with both barrels.

But the one thing we did have in common was that we both appreciated Paul Krause. Paul played in the College All-Star game that first year and arrived to camp late. Right away we both knew that this guy had talent. In his rookie year Krause led the entire NFL with 12 interceptions. It would have been 14, but two were nullified.

As the offensive unit would be exiting the field, I would always make it a point that the defense be coming on. I was the first guy in the huddle because I was the one who called the signals. This one time I was just about to call a defense when I noticed that Paul was not there. I looked up and there he was wandering on to the field, just taking his time. I was livid, to say the least. "Let me tell you something, Krause. I've been playing this game a hell of a lot longer than you and I've never been the last guy in the huddle. That better be the last time for you. I don't care how many interceptions you've got. Start acting like you want to hit somebody and play!"

Paul never said a word and he was never again late to a huddle. He went on to become an All-Pro and we became very good friends.

The '64 Season

The '64 season began with four straight losses. We opened the regular season at home against the Browns and lost 27–13. Our next two games were away. The first was against the Cowboys in Dallas, final score: 24–18. The second was against the Giants in New York, final score: 13–10.

That first game against the Giants was in New York and was an extremely emotional one for me. It was the home opener at Yankee Stadium and I wanted the win more than I had ever wanted anything in my life. Before the game I was introduced to the crowd and was given a long, standing ovation. After the game I visited the Giant locker room and their clubhouse man, Pete Sheehy. Pete had worked for the Yankees since the 1920s and paid me one of the greatest compliments I ever received. "You know, Sam, I have been here since the days of Ruth and Gehrig and that ovation was equal to anything I've ever heard for the Yankees."

Those words helped ease some of the pain from a loss that never should have been.

It was late in the game and we were leading New York 10–6. Tittle had been injured with broken ribs that he had received against the Steelers a week prior, and a young quarterback out of Cornell, Gary Wood, had taken his place. Wood was 0-for-10 in passing in the first half.

Late in the game we held on to that four-point lead; that was, until Charley Taylor fumbled the ball deep in Redskin territory. New York recovered and drove the ball to the goal line. With fourth-and-1 and the game on the line, I knew the ball would go to Alex Webster. Sure enough, the ball was snapped and Alex was the intended receiver, but Wood missed the handoff. I was already keyed in on Webster and hit him just short of the goal line. Meanwhile, Wood had no alternative but to hold on to the ball and go in for the score. Final score: Giants 13, Redskins 10.

To say that I was devastated is an understatement. I was so furious that I ran off the field, set my sights on Allie Sherman and gave him a shot from the side. I neither hurt him nor knocked him down, and as I look back on what I had done, it was really stupid. But the emotions and frustrations of losing that game had taken their toll.

All in all, the team was beginning to show promise. But poor Sonny, the crowd was merciless and booed him every time he stepped foot on the field. Then, in Week 5, the jeers turned to praise, and Sonny even managed to quiet his critics. Jurgensen completed 22 passes for 385 yards, beating the Eagles 35–20. Sonny also got the chance to prove that the trade the Redskins made to get him was the right move. The Washington player who was traded for Jurgensen was Norm Snead, the new Eagles' quarterback.

We went on to win five of our final eight games, including a big win over the Cowboys 28–16, and a huge, personal win over the Giants and Allie Sherman 36–21. We finished the season 6–8–0 and finished third in the Eastern Division. Overall, I was impressed with what the team had accomplished, and was optimistic about the future.

I also took a lot of satisfaction from the Giants' 2–10–2 season. I knew that Sherman would take a lot of heat, which he rightfully deserved.

A Dismal '65 Season

I truly believed that the 1965 Redskins would be a contender. McPeak's contract had been renewed, and through trades we picked up a veteran fullback from the Bears by the name of Rick Casares, guard Darrell Dess from the Giants, and Lions defensive end Bill Quinlan. We scored big in the draft by picking up Arizona State tight end Jerry Smith and Arizona defensive back Rickie Harris, and a little known linebacker from North Carolina who showed up in the 18th round, Chris Hanburger.

Chris wasn't that big and had mostly played the center position at North Carolina. Once McPeak had seen the talent that this kid had displayed during drills, there was no doubt that his days at playing center were over. Ed Hughes worked with Hanburger on playing linebacker. With Chris playing outside and me playing inside, we made a great team. Hanburger could run sideline to sideline, but when it came to tackling he was really bad. His technique was wrong and I would always get on him. He would use his hands to pull a defender down instead of driving his shoulder into the ball carrier. But during the final two years of my career, I was the one getting knocked down and Chris wouldn't let me forget it. He would say, "If you're such a great tackler, how come I'm always scraping you off the field?"

And he was right!

Well, the season didn't open up as we had expected. As a matter of fact, it was downright horrible. After losing our first two games against Cleveland and Dallas and scoring only 14 points for both games, McPeak decided to start second-year quarterback Dick Shiner over Jurgensen. Sonny was irate, and when we lost our third game to the Lions, McPeak still went with Shiner the following week.

We were losing to the Cardinals by a large margin when the coach summoned Sonny to go in late in the game. Sonny blatantly refused. "You wanted to go with Shiner, you made your choice. I'm not going in."

Our losing streak continued with losses to the Cardinals and the Colts, giving us an 0–5 record. Finally Edward Bennett Williams called for a team meeting. He came out to D.C. Stadium, asked the coaches to leave the room, and began his spiel. "We've lost five straight and we've spent a lot of money on this football team. We've got a lot of great players out there and I'd like to know what's going on. I want to lay it all on the table and find out what's wrong here."

The response that Williams received was not exactly what he had expected. First we heard from Bill Quinlan, who'd come over from Detroit but who had also spent three years with the Packers. "Mr. Williams, when I was with Green Bay, we partied a lot, we drank a lot, and we won a lot. The trouble with this team is we don't drink enough around here."

I really don't think that that was what Williams had in mind, but it gets better. Mean John Paluck got up and said, "What Quinlan here says isn't exactly true. I've been here a lot of years and I can tell you we've drunk enough and partied enough to be world champions."

Williams could do nothing but laugh. What the hell, we were already 0–5 and our season was pretty much over. I think that talk actually cleared the air, and I'll be goddamned if we didn't start playing better.

The following week we beat the Cardinals 24–20, Sonny threw for three touchdowns and Williams was presented with the game ball. In the next four weeks we went on to beat the Eagles, the Giants, and the Steelers, losing only to the Eagles on the road. Next up were the Dallas Cowboys, who had come a long way since their inaugural year.

We were trailing 21–0 early in the second quarter. The Cowboys then owner, Clint Murchison, was so convinced that Dallas would win that he left at the half to fly home to Texas. Big mistake on his part.

Late in the second quarter Charley Taylor scored on a 26-yard pass from Sonny, but the PAT failed and the score was 21–6. In the third quarter, Sonny rushed in from the 1-yard line, making the score 24–13. In the fourth Dan Lewis rushed for a two-yard TD, making the score 24–20. The excitement was short lived when Sonny threw an interception, and Don Meredith came in and threw 35 yards to Frank Clarke for the score. The Cowboys went ahead 31–20, but not for long. Sonny threw to a 10-yard pass to Bobby Mitchell for six points and with four minutes remaining in the game, hit Angelo Coia in the end zone making the score 34–31. But there was still 1:12 remaining in the game. Meredith came in and drove the Cowboys down the field. We finally stopped them when Dallas' field goal kicker Danny Villanueva set up to kick a 44-yard field goal. He never got the kick off. Fred Williams and I opened a hole in the line while Lonnie Sanders came through to block the kick. Final score 34–31, Redskins. Sonny completed 26 of 42 passes for 411 yards and became the hero of D.C. But unfortunately, it wasn't enough.

We lost the next two games to Cleveland and New York, and although we beat the Steelers in our final game of the season, it was too little too late. With a 6–8–0 season and finishing fourth in the Eastern Division, some major changes would be made within the organization.

Edward Bennett Williams fired McPeak at the end of the '65 season and began his quest for a new head coach. On January 25, 1966, former Cleveland Browns quarterback and Hall of Famer Otto Graham was named head coach and general manager of the Redskins.

It would be downhill for Washington until 1969.

Next Stop: Vietnam

A few weeks prior to Otto being officially hired, I received a call from Williams. My first thought was that I had been traded again. His cheerful voice on the other end of the line said, "I've got good news for you, Sam. The Defense Department has arranged for you, Frank Gifford, John Unitas, and Willie Davis to take a two-week trip to Vietnam. You will tour the country, visit the troops out in the fields and spend time at the bases and hospitals."

I was a little concerned about flying off to Southeast Asia. By this time, the war had escalated. Regardless, I considered it an honor to be chosen to go. Mary even seemed to find some humor in it all. "Gee, Sam. It sounds like you won a contest called 'The Linebacker We'd Most Like to Send to War.' Who nominated you, Jim Brown or Jimmy Taylor?"

Within a few weeks I was off to Saigon. It took 23 hours to get there. Officials met us at the plane and we were immediately driven to our hotel, no stops in between. The entire area was surrounded by barbed wire and Marine guards were stationed behind sandbags on the sidewalk in front of the hotel.

By that afternoon, we were briefed on what to expect, given fatigues and an ID badge to wear. The ID badge had the word "Non-combatant" written on it. Willie Davis looked at the badge then looked at the officer who had given it to us and said, "Hell, man, this badge is no damned good. It's in English. How are those VC going to know what it means?"

The officer replied, "Don't worry, Willie. If they get that close to you, they won't give you time to get your badge out of your pocket."

With that, the reality of being in a war zone quickly set in. Willie asked if he could be issued a gun. The officer responded with, "They'll shoot you faster if you've got a weapon."

Later that day we were given the VIP tour of Saigon. Talk about a rude awakening. My God! The poverty, the stench of garbage and raw sewage, and the living conditions were absolutely appalling. As we drove through the congested streets I questioned one of the soldiers who were assigned to us how they knew who the enemy was. By this time we were all outfitted in military attire and looked just like the other American soldiers. His replay was frightening. "Any one of 'em could be the enemy. See that guy over there? Well, if he walks up here and shakes you hand, he's a friend of yours. If he walks up here and shoots you, then he's the enemy."

The following day we visited a field hospital at Tan Son Nhut airport, located outside of Saigon. This was the final stop for the wounded before they were flown home. On our way there we passed three trucks carrying South Korean soldiers. This specific group of military personnel was considered to be one of the most vicious and brutal units in the war. We had just passed them when someone threw a firecracker at one of the trucks. Within moments there was total mayhem. The Koreans immediately leaped from the truck and opened fire. They leveled everything in sight. Luckily no one was hurt, but it was quite obvious that we were all deeply shaken by the incident.

As I mentioned before, I get sick to my stomach just thinking about getting a shot, and here I was about to enter a field hospital with victims of war who have been wounded, amputated, and maimed. These men were kids, not much older than my son Sam Jr., and they had already been to hell and back.

There were also a few veterans in that ward. One of those vets was a sergeant—a 14-year veteran who had stepped on a land mine that had blown away half of his face. He was bandaged from head to toe. I was extremely moved and found it difficult to speak to him, but managed to get out a few words. "Sarge, I hate to see you like this. It's a privilege to meet you. You don't have to say anything. Just hang in there."

Talk about a tough soldier. He looked at me and spoke through his bandages. "Hell. I can still talk. Just got messed up a little."

All of a sudden I developed an attitude change. Who the hell was I to bitch with all this misery and suffering around me? It was then that I truly realized my purpose for being here. It was for the troops, for those boys and men who risked their lives for us. I took a good look at myself and said, "If you don't have the guts or the nerve or whatever it takes to go through a hospital, well, you've got to be a bigger person than that."

I made it my personal mission to do the job that I was sent there to do, but I have to admit, it was never easy. It was difficult for all of us. Gifford was especially having a hard time dealing with the grief and despair of these brave men.

The entire time we were in Vietnam, we were never shot at, but that's not to say that we didn't experience some terrifying things. I never did get used to landing on an aircraft carrier. It scared the hell out of me. Assault landings were even worse. They were designed to evade enemy gunfire. The plane would fly into the area at an altitude that was out of enemy fire range, then suddenly plunge down at what felt like goddamned mach speed.

One morning we were flying to a Special Forces base of operations located in Quang Ngai when the plane began to make its descent. Suddenly we began to nosedive and Willie Davis said I was clutching his leg so tight that I almost broke it. I turned around to look at Gifford and his face was crimson.

Frank took a lot of heat from the guys on that trip. Mr. Hollywood, as Jim Lee Howell used to call him, was in the World War II Warner Brothers movie, *Darby's Rangers*. We kept reminding him that this wasn't a film and we didn't break for lunch between battles.

We visited 22 different venues in those 12 days. I learned something about myself during that time. You know how fans talk about how tough football players are? Well, I'll tell you, it is nothing compared to what these guys had gone through in combat. They are the real tough guys. They are the real heroes.

My Vietnam experience stayed with me for a very long time. My life seemed to somehow change. All of a sudden, football didn't seem so important anymore.

A New Season, A New Coach

Otto Graham took over as head coach for the 1966 campaign. He was a great guy and very personable, but he seemed a little too relaxed to be a successful head coach in the NFL. Granted, he was a great quarterback for the Cleveland Browns, and he had a mind for the game, but I always had the feeling that coaching wasn't really his forte. He never seemed to be organized and spent far more time with the offense than with the defense. That quickly turned the job over to Ed Hughes.

Unlike previous years, practices were long and boring and I soon began to despise training camp. In the past, I always looked forward to it, now I couldn't wait to leave.

I was also concerned about the fact that Otto had yet to develop a game plan. Our first preseason game was against Johnny Unitas and the Colts at D.C. Stadium, and throughout the entire week of practice, Baltimore was never even mentioned. We didn't even have a scouting report.

I decided to go and have a talk with Otto, and find out what the hell was going on. I confronted him in his office and he said, "Sam, I'm probably a little different kind of coach than you're used to. I don't think you can keep ballplayers motivated for a full season, so what I want to do is play a lot of people in this first game. You're not going to play much. Neither is Sonny. I know what you guys can do, and I want to see some of the younger guys. When I cut a man, I want to make sure he gets a fair shake."

Otto's plan was for Sonny and me to only play the first quarter. Never in my life have I only played one quarter, and now I would be sitting on the bench watching a great team that none of us knew anything about.

Of course we were annihilated by the Colts 35–0. Sonny and I only played two series in the entire first quarter and Otto made it a point to play everybody. To say that Graham was a different kind of coach was an understatement, and that was proven right off the bat during the college draft. A soccer-style kicker from Princeton by the name of Charlie Gogolak was the Redskins' first round pick. The reasoning behind this was the idea of Edward Bennett Williams. He said he was sick and tired of every extra point being an adventure.

I still consider it a bad move, and no one in the history of football has ever used a No. 1 draft pick on a kicker. In 1979 the Saints went against conventional wisdom when they chose kicker/punter Russell Erxleben as the 11th pick in the first round of the draft. To this day, with the exception of Gogolak, no kicker has ever been drafted higher than Erxleben.

What made things even more difficult was that Charlie wasn't exactly well liked by the guys. He was extremely intelligent, but I never saw his desire or passion for the game. Williams took an immediate liking to him, especially when he found out Charlie's intention to go to law school. And needless to say, the Redskins definitely helped with his tuition. When Gogolak signed with the Redskins he was given a huge salary, plus bonuses. Not bad for a guy who hardly practiced and only kicked for 5 or 10 minutes a day.

I'm sure Charlie knew how we felt and that most of us were not happy with the Redskins using their top draft pick for a kicker.

Joe Don Looney—A Man True to His Name

The rest of the draft wasn't that great either. We did, however, acquire a few good players from trades and waivers. Our safety, Jim Steffen, was sent to the Cowboys in exchange for defensive back Brig Owens, offensive tackle Mitch Johnson, and offensive guard Jake Kupp. Once the season started, the Giants sent us linebacker Jim Carroll and running back Steve Thurlow. But the most fascinating acquisition of all came from Detroit (via New York and Baltimore) when they sent us a 6'1", 230-pound running back by the name of Joe Don Looney, a man true to his name.

Looney had been the Giants' No. 1 draft pick in 1964, the year that I was traded. My former roommate, Don Chandler, had told me all about him. Looney and Chandler became roommates after I left, Chandler being from Tulsa and Looney being from Oklahoma.

The Redskins were scheduled to play an exhibition game against the Giants at Cornell. When I arrived in Ithaca, I met with Chandler. He immediately began to talk to me about Looney. "Sam, he's crazy! You've never met anyone like him! I just can't figure him out!"

Don had just finished his sentence when Joe Don walked into the room. The guy was huge. He had movie-star looks, like Burt Reynolds, except much, much bigger. He wore a T-shirt, blue jeans, and sandals. He had a muscular physique unlike anything I'd ever seen. We began talking and I told him how lucky he was to be playing with such a great organization and in such a great city. His reply was not exactly what I had expected. "Great? I hate this place! These coaches don't know what they're doing. I'm hurt, and they make me come up here to this game. Shofner's back in New York. He's hurt, he didn't have to make this trip. I got a sore leg. I can't play. I can't run. I ought to be back in the city."

I had spoken with Y.A. Tittle and he told me that Joe Don didn't want to practice. The coaches asked Y.A. to go and talk to him, figuring he would have respect for a veteran quarterback. Wrong. He just laughed at Y.A.

Even Wellington Mara went to his room and tried to get him to come out. Once again, Joe Don refused. Wellington slipped a note under his door that said he would be fined $200 if he didn't show up for practice. Looney returned the note (under the door) and wrote the words, "Make it $250."

Looney's lunacy got him traded to Baltimore, which traded him to Detroit. One day Otto called Sonny and me into his office. He let us know that the organization was considering contracting Joe Don with the Redskins. "We need a strong running back to complement Charley Taylor and A. D. Whitfield."

I remembered my conversation with Looney and immediately began to shake my head. I had this to say to Otto. "First of all, three of the best organizations in football wanted no part of this guy. What makes the Redskins think they could change this guy? We have enough guys on this team who are a little weird. Why do we need another one?"

Sonny thoroughly agreed. But it was obvious that the decision had already been made, and I had a strong feeling that once again Edward Bennett Williams was behind it. The so-called logic of it all was that he was a No. 1 draft choice, a big name, and Washington could get him cheap. Joe Don reported to camp.

Within a few short days, Otto called me into his office. He realized that he needed someone to babysit Joe Don on the road. He asked me if I would mind rooming with him. "Yes, I would! Sonny and I get along real well, and I am in no mood to babysit Looney."

Otto must have known my answer because he was already willing to make it worth my while. "If you room with him and keep him out of trouble, we will give you a $1,500 bonus."

That immediately got my attention, and the following week I began rooming with Joe Don. Not only did I acquire a new roommate, but also a major pain in the ass.

"Taking care" of Joe Don was not an easy task. His looks and build, alone, attracted women from all over. I remember this one time when we were staying at the Mayflower Hotel in downtown Washington. That was where the team stayed the night before every home game. This one particular night, Joe Don had gone to the coffee shop. I stayed in my room and was watching *Gunsmoke* on TV when I heard a knock at the door.

I answered the door and a beautiful woman said she was looking for Joe Don. She wanted to come in, but I told her that Looney wasn't here. She said she had come all the way from Delaware to spend the night with him. I almost fell over.

I assured her that she definitely had the right room, but I still wasn't going to let her in. Just then Joe Don came into the room and told her to stick around. He turned and looked at me and said, "Just give me 10 minutes."

I told him it wasn't going to happen. Bed check was about to begin and I wasn't about to lose $1,500 for a ten-minute roll in the hay. She finally left and my bonus was saved.

Another problem with Looney was that he had trouble sleeping. When he didn't sleep, I didn't sleep. One night we were at the Mayflower and Joe Don got up at three o'clock in the morning and opened the window. My first thought was that he was going to jump. I bolted out of bed and started yelling, "Don't jump, Joe Don, don't jump!"

He looked at me as though I was the nut in the room and said, "What are you talking about, Sam? I'm just trying to get a little fresh air."

I managed to live through that first season with him, but it wasn't as easy the following year. We had been practicing at D.C. Stadium for our opener against the Eagles. We were dressed in full gear and the humid September weather began to get to us. The team was hot and tired, but Otto insisted that we keep practicing.

In one of our drills, the offense was running Eagle plays for the defense. We were supposed to run at half-speed and not hit anyone. In this particular play a back would run through the hole and all you were supposed to do is get into position, touch him, and let him go. Joe Don got the call. He got a pitchout then cut back inside and hit the hole. I pursued the play, positioned myself to make the tackle, and stopped, like we were supposed to do in a half-speed drill. The only problem was that Joe Don decided to go full speed and not stop.

He lowered his shoulder and ran over me. He hit me so hard in the chest with his shoulder pads that I was literally airborne and propelled five yards back. As I was lying there in a daze, he shoved the football in my face and said, "How'd you like that, big boy? I knocked the crap out of you!"

To say that I was furious would be an understatement. I yelled back, "Psycho! You just picked on the wrong guy!"

I knew Joe Don would get the ball on the next play. They would run a trap and he would come right up the middle. My friend, center Len Hauss knew it too. He also knew that I was steaming mad, so he just got out of the way and didn't even try to block me.

Just before the ball was snapped, Joe Don stood there in that cocky stance, with his hands on his hips, looked my way, and blurted out, "Here I come again, big boy. Let's see what you really got!"

As he came through the hole I was there to meet him. I hit him with everything I had. The popping of the pads could be heard for miles. His headgear flew one way and the ball flew another. Joe Don came after me and we began to fight. It was a real slugfest and Otto didn't know what to do. No one could separate us. Joe Don was screaming and yelling at me, "I'll kill you, Huff. I'll bomb your house!"

During that brawl, I was just as crazy as he was.

Well, obviously we never roomed together again and to tell you the truth, I could have cared less about the $1,500. It wasn't worth the stress and frustration of living with a madman.

Sadly enough though, Joe Don's life ended tragically. After his five-team, five-year NFL career ended, this maverick and misfit served three tours in Vietnam. In September of 1988, while riding his motorcycle, Joe Don failed to make a curve and was thrown off his bike and killed instantly. He was only 45 years old.

The Absent-Minded Professor

Otto was never the disciplinarian type. He was more like the absent-minded professor type. I remember when our receiver Preston Carpenter was caught breaking curfew. The following day we were playing the Browns and Carpenter dropped a perfect pass in the end zone. We ended up losing the game and Otto was clearly upset. He called Sonny and me in to discuss how much we should fine Preston. I said $500, while Sonny voted for $250. Otto decided on $1,000. He then looked at both of us and said, "It if had been either one of you guys, it would have been $5,000 a piece."

At training camp you could find him out on the tennis courts. That should tell you something right there. He was one of the worst dressers you ever wanted to see. He would wear a porkpie hat with mismatched clothes. He never wore a tie. In fact, all he ever wore were polo shirts, golf pants, white socks, and Hush Puppies. Not exactly a fashion plate. During practice Otto had a habit of slapping his clipboard. The players used to bet on how many times he would do it walking from the locker room to the practice field.

Personally, I liked Otto Graham, but I always had the feeling that he didn't really care for the professional game anymore. There was one day, though, where he really pissed me off. He called me into his office and said, "Sam, on the field you are a great captain, but off the field, I don't think you're much."

"What the hell are you talking about, Otto?" I always prided myself on living a decent, quiet life.

Otto sat up in his chair at his desk and said, "I'm talking about after practice. When I say practice is over, you and John Reger are always the first guys off the field. I don't think that's right and if it happens again, I'm going to fine you."

"Wait a minute, Otto. You mean that when you say practice is over, you mean practice is *not* over?"

"That's right! Jerry Smith and a lot of other guys stay out there and work on their pass patterns. So I want you guys there, too. Don't be heading for the barn."

So from that day forward, Reger and I stayed out on the field. When Gogolak would come out to practice his five minutes of kicking, John would shag the ball, throw it to me, and I would throw it to the center. Talk about a waste of time, but it made Otto happy and kept him from fining us.

1966: The Graham Era

We lost our first two regular-season games. The Browns beat us at home 38–14, and the Cardinals crushed us on their home turf 23–7. President Lyndon Johnson was in attendance for the Browns game. He watched us lose from up in Ed Williams' private suite while Otto made a statement to the press that didn't sit well with the White House, "Maybe the President will stay home next time."

We did, however, go on to beat the Steelers in consecutive weeks (33–27 and 24–10), the Falcons 33–20, and the Cardinals 26–20, losing only to the Giants by a score of 13–10. But it was during that week of practice—right before we played the Cardinals—that Otto made one of the greatest moves in NFL franchise history. He switched running back Charley Taylor to the wide receiver position. At the time, the future Hall of Fame player wasn't too happy about the move, but in the long run it saved his legs and prolonged his NFL career. When he retired in 1977, Charley had caught more passes than any other receiver in the history of the National Football League.

One of the reasons for the switch was because our offensive line was too slow for Taylor to follow. He was so quick that he made most of his yards on his own. When our guards pulled out on a sweep and before they could hit their opponents, Charley was already well out in front of them.

In Week 8 we beat the Eagles 27–13, giving us a 5–3 record, but we ended up losing our next three games to Baltimore 37–10, Dallas 31–30, and Cleveland 14–3. But in Week 12, the gods were definitely shining down upon us.

The day was Sunday, November 27. The Washington Redskins were about to face the New York Giants at D.C. Stadium. For the Giants and Allie Sherman, it would be a long and sour day, but for me, vengeance and retribution would finally be meted out.

The Giants defense was worse than ours. They were giving up more points than any other team in the history of the game. In my opinion, the '66 Giants under the tutelage of that egotistical jerk Allie Sherman were the epitome of inferior professional football. Prior to the game Sonny asked me how many points we needed. With faith and confidence that the Redskins could do the job, I responded with, "Sonny, you'll score 60."

He thought I was crazy, but I'd been studying the films. Hell, they'd played the Rams two weeks before and gave up 55 points. There was no doubt in my mind whatsoever that Sonny would light 'em up.

Former Giants quarterback Kyle Rote was now a sports broadcaster and hosted his own pregame radio show. We were on the field before the game when he interviewed me. "What do you think about the game, Sam?"

I brought the microphone up to my mouth for all my friends in New York to hear. "The Rams may have scored 55 points against the Giants, but we'll score 60."

As I walked back to where the team was warming up, Otto asked me my thoughts about how the game would go. "Otto, we're gonna kill 'em!" I never in my life said that to a head coach, but I really believed it. "And Otto, I want to ask you one more thing. Show no mercy. Show no mercy to that so-called coach across the field, because this is our day."

My predictions about our offense came true, but our damned defense was practically comatose. By the end of the third quarter we had allowed the Giants to score four touchdowns. In my book, that was four too many. As Sonny came off the field, he stopped and said, "Jesus, Sam, how many more times do I have to score?"

My answer: "Don't let up. Just don't let up."

Finally, by the fourth quarter, our defense began to show some signs of life. The Redskins scored three more times and took the lead 69–41. The game was down to the final seconds and we were just going to let the clock run down. It was fourth down and we were on the Giant 22-yard line. Timeout was called with seven seconds remaining in the game. While Otto was talking to Sonny, I took it upon myself to get the field-goal unit out on the field. Before Otto or Sonny even realized what had happened, Gogolak kicked a 29-yard field goal to beat the Giants 72–41.

Otto took a lot of heat for running up the score. When he was questioned by the sportswriters as to why he didn't just kill the clock, he said, "Gogolak needed the practice."

But you have to remember that Otto didn't make the decision to go for the field goal—I did. Those 72 points that we scored were for all the people who got screwed by Allie Sherman: Mo, Livingston, Rosey, all the old Giant players, and me. In my mind, this was retribution day for Allie Sherman, and justice was finally mine.

The following week saw us squeeze by Dallas 34–31, only to lose our last game of the season to the Eagles 37–28. We finished a disappointing 7–7.

1967: The Biggest Mistake of My Life

The 1967 season saw Sonny finishing the year with over 3,700 yards passing, Charley Taylor and Jerry Smith finished first and second in the league in receiving, and Bobby Mitchell was fourth. Despite missing three games with an injury, Charley was still able to lead the league in receiving.

1967 may have been a good year for those four, but for me, it became a year for injury. I had never been injured badly enough to miss a game in all my years with the NFL until then.

On Sunday, October 22, we faced the Rams in Los Angeles. Our record up until then was 2–2–1 with victories over the Saints and Giants, losses to the Eagles and Cowboys, and a 20–20 tie with the Falcons.

The Rams' coach was George Allen and his quarterback was a 6'5", 220-pound, first-round draft choice out of North Carolina State back in 1962. His name was Roman Gabriel. Gabriel wasn't what one would consider a smooth runner. He didn't always know where he was going to run. That, along with his size, made him difficult to bring down. It was here that the problem occurred.

Early in the game Gabriel tried to dodge me by scrambling upfield. It put me a little off balance. Just then our 6'4", 275-pound defensive tackle Spain Musgrove hit Gabriel from behind. In the process my foot got caught underneath Spain as he fell to the ground, causing it to bend backward. The pain was excruciating. It was a miracle that the leg didn't break, but the tendons around my right ankle had completely ripped. George Resta, our team doctor, and Joe Kuczo, our trainer, said it was the worst ankle injury they'd ever witnessed.

I ended up missing five games that season. I was given cortisone shots and heat treatments to help me get the ankle back to normal, but I couldn't even walk without limping, much less play in a game. Our defense wasn't all that good when I was playing and now with me on injured reserve, they were absolutely awful.

Week 12 finally came around and I was cleared to play against the Eagles, but Ed Hughes didn't put me in till the third quarter. Philly had moved down the field toward our goal line and Ed, on the side of caution, figured that I wouldn't have to move very far. As I jogged to the huddle, the crowd gave me a standing ovation. That was an incredible thrill for me. After being down 35–28 at the end of the third quarter, we came back to tie the Eagles 35–35 on a score by our rookie running back out of Cornell, Pete Larson.

I continued to play the rest of the season in a great deal of pain. I dreaded Tuesdays the most. That's when Dr. Resta would come to practice to give me my cortisone injection. I would go into the training room so the players wouldn't hear me screaming when I saw that damned needle. Hell, it looked like it was a foot long. Dr. Resta would inject the cortisone directly into the joint, and was it ever painful.

All in all, the 1967 season was depressing. Otto's coaching had gotten to me and I was hurting and could barely walk. It seemed that everywhere I turned people were telling me that maybe it was time to hang up my cleats. "We don't want to see you get hurt. You've been a great player; don't just hang on for the paycheck."

It wasn't long till I began to believe them.

A few days prior to our final game of the season, I asked our publicity person, Joe Blair, to call a press conference. When practice was over I saw the media waiting for me. There were local camera crews, the networks and even a few broadcasters from New York.

I walked directly into the Redskins' dressing room and sat down in front of my locker. My entire career flashed through my mind. I glanced up at my pads and helmet and suddenly realized that I would never again suit up for a game. I started crying right there in front of the entire team.

Many of the guys didn't know how to react. One of them went into Otto's office and told him that I was crying. Otto came over and sat down next to me. He put his hand on my shoulder and said, "Sam, everybody gets old."

"Thanks, Otto."

I finally composed myself and met with the press, but the composure didn't last long. Once again, I broke down.

Washington Post sportswriter Dave Brady wrote this about my retiring from football:

"Tears flowed like champagne at a championship celebration as the Redskins inched up and gave Sam Huff an understanding squeeze on the shoulder."

The decision to retire really didn't hit me until the following year. It was then that I realized that I had made the biggest mistake of my life.

1969: Reunited With Lombardi

My family and I moved back to the New York area—actually it was Franklin Lakes, New Jersey, in Bergen County. I went back to work for J.P. Stevens. Even though I enjoyed what I did, there seemed to be something missing, something that kept eating away at me, and the closer it got to training camp, the worse I began to feel. I finally admitted to myself that I still loved the game and missed the excitement and camaraderie of it all. But little did I know that a second chance at playing the game that I so dearly loved would come my way in the form of a great friend and an even greater coach.

After leading the Redskins through another losing season, Graham was released as head coach at the end of the '68 campaign. Not only did Otto finish the year with a 5–9–0 record, but he also traded our great defensive back, Paul Krause, to Minnesota for reserve tight end, Marlin McKeever. Needless to say, the fans were not happy, and Edward Bennett Williams, looking for a big name to replace Otto, found the biggest name of all: Vince Lombardi.

Williams had tried several times in the past to get Lombardi to come to Washington. When Bill McPeak was fired in 1965, Lombardi's name had come up as head coach, but the job went to Graham. By 1968 Vince had relinquished his coaching position with the Packers and went on to become the team's general manager. Lombardi was never happy being in the front office. He belonged on the field with the players and when Williams offered him the coaching position and a percentage of Redskins stock, Vince jumped at the chance.

On February 7, 1969, Vince Lombardi became the 16th coach of the Washington Redskins' franchise. Williams also made him the general manager. At the press conference that day, Lombardi told the media, "I can't walk across the Potomac."

But none of the reporters believed him.

A few weeks prior to Vince getting the job, I met him and his wife Marie on a flight from New York. Marie had offered me her seat next to Vince and we began to talk. "I hear you're talking to the Redskins about coaching the team," I said.

"There's a real good chance that I will get the job. We're trying to put the deal together now."

At that point I was seriously thinking about leaving the business world and getting back into football and eventually becoming a head coach with one of the NFL teams. "Coach, if you ever do get the job, I would really love to coach for you."

Lombardi looked at me and smiled. "I'll keep that in mind, Sam."

Vince called me in New Jersey a few days after accepting the head coaching position. "Sam, I was thinking about our conversation on the plane. I've had some second thoughts about it. I've got somebody else in mind to coach the defense. He's got a little more coaching experience than you do. I was referring to Harland Svare."

Harland was my former teammate, and I told Vince that I thought he would be a good choice. Then I made him another offer, one I was hoping he wouldn't refuse. "How about letting me work with the linebackers under Harland, and I'll be a player/coach?"

That caught his attention. "You think you can play another year?"

"Yes, sir, I know I can," I quickly replied.

Without hesitation Lombardi set the wheels in motion. "Well, I need to buy some time with this team. If you can give me one year, we can develop some guys behind you, and that just might work out. Why don't you come down to Washington and we'll talk about it."

The irony of this whole thing was that I had just seen a film at a company sales meeting called *Second Effort*. It was a motivational movie starring Lombardi. After viewing it I really began to think that I could still play. In the meantime, the people at J.P. Stevens were trying to talk me out of leaving, but after meeting with Vince and being passed over for a promotion, my mind was made up. I decided to resign my position and resume my football career.

I flew to Washington to meet with Lombardi at the Redskins' office. He came right to the point. "Now, Sam, I run a very tough training camp. Much tougher than anything you may remember in New York. If you want to play, you'll have to do everything everyone else does."

I guaranteed him that it wouldn't be a problem. Hell, I kept thinking about Sonny and that old gut of his. If he could get through it, it would be a piece of cake for me. Besides, I'd heard all the horror stories about Vince, but I figured he couldn't be that tough. Boy, was I wrong.

In all my years in football, I never saw a man drive people harder than Vince Lombardi. He would yell and scream at you at the top of his lungs. But he knew when to stop and build you back up. There was also a warm side to Vince. Each day at the end of training camp he and the assistant coaches would meet for a beer or two with the press before dinner. The talks were all off the record, and Lombardi relished the give and take of the conversation. Vince could be very charming when he wanted to. He was also very religious. He went so far as to house a priest in the dorm at training camp so he wouldn't have to take time to go to church for morning Mass.

I really loved Vince, but I feared him more than any man in my life. And now the Washington Redskins would soon learn and experience the wrath of Lombardi.

Fullback Ray McDonald

Ray McDonald was a 6'4", 248-pound fullback who was the Redskins' No. 1 draft pick out of Idaho in 1967. To look at him, you would have said that he epitomized the look of a professional football player, but his skills and talent fell far short. I didn't know Ray that well, but I knew that he would have problems making the cut.

Prior to the start of the '69 season, the coaching staff was accessing its personnel when Lombardi asked me what I thought of Ray McDonald. "He's just not a football player."

Lombardi yelled back, "What do you mean? We had him rated real high when I was in Green Bay. He's a No. 1 draft choice, so how can he not be a player?"

I looked at Vince and said, "Coach, he's not going to be the kind of player you want. If you're looking for another Jimmy Taylor or another Paul Hornung, you've got the wrong guy."

Vince snapped back, "We'll just see about that, mister. We'll just see."

Lombardi never let you forget that he was in charge, but in this situation he realized that I was right.

Ray was constantly in the training room. He complained that the Achilles tendon injury that he received the year before still bothered him. During practice, Lombardi was all over him. Ray knew he was in serious trouble and might not make the team. His strategy? Ray came up with a pulled leg muscle.

Every night at seven o'clock we had a team meeting. Remember, we all had to run on Lombardi time, which was 15 minutes prior to the meeting time. The players had better be in their seats by 6:45. Ray sauntered into the room at five to seven. Lombardi screamed at him, "Get up front here, mister. There are plenty of seats up front. By the way, mister, you're late, and that will be a $75 fine."

McDonald walked to the front row and sat down. "I'm not late, Coach. It's five minutes to seven."

Vince was furious. "I said you were late, mister, and not only are you late, you're also hurt, isn't that right?"

"Yes, sir."

"And did you see the doctor today?"

"No sir, I didn't."

Lombardi was outraged and began screaming at McDonald in front of the team. "You're fired! Just get the hell out of this room, you disgrace the Green Bay Packer uniform!"

Just then I leaned over and whispered, "Coach, that's the Redskins uniform."

Lombardi screamed, "You disgrace the Redskin uniform, so get out of here! Go play for the Roanoke Buckskins or whatever the hell they call themselves. But you will never wear this uniform again, mister. You're fired!"

Never in my entire football career had I ever seen that done to a player. The room went silent and no one dared say a word. The wrath of Lombardi was beyond belief.

A Method to His Madness

One of our assistant coaches, Don Doll, ran the calisthenics segment of the workouts. When I say calisthenics, I'm not talking jumping jacks. Hell, I thought he was trying to kill us. He had us doing leg lifts, push-ups, and duck walks. Just when you thought you would die, Lombardi would take over and run you ragged through the grass drills. They were the true torture of the workouts.

You would begin with running in place, then Vince would holler, "On your belly!" or "On your back!" You would immediately hit the dirt then pop up when he yelled, "On your feet!" We repeated that at least 15 to 20 times. Each time Vince would be checking Sonny and me to see that we weren't doggin' it. When we looked as if we were going to die, Lombardi would stop the drill.

Following the grass drills, we would all run a lap around the field—about a quarter of a mile. God help you if you were last. I remember telling Chris Hanburger and Harold McLinton that if they had to carry me, then do so, but be sure that I wasn't last.

After sustaining two weeks of physical torture, Sonny and I dropped a lot of weight. Sonny completely lost his belly. But at the coaches' meeting, Lombardi was still complaining that the team wasn't in shape.

"Hell, when they come back from that run, all these guys have their hands on their knees and they're breathing too heavy. I've always believed that most games are won in the last two minutes and the team that's in the best condition will win those games. No team is going to out-condition mine."

The next day I passed the word around to my teammates that they were not to look as if they were dying when they finished the run. Guys were taking deep breaths and walking around and some even had a tinge of blue to their face, but no one had their hands on their knees. In reality, they actually began to look like a well-conditioned team. That evening Lombardi had a smile on his face.

"We're getting there, we're getting there. They're finally getting in shape."

But in typical Lombardi fashion, that smile didn't last long.

One day at practice Vince wasn't happy with his team's performance of the grass drills. He brought the defensive linemen up front where he could see them. As if the drills weren't already tough, Lombardi decided to add a few more. All of a sudden our big defensive end Bill Briggs started throwing up all over the field. As Briggs lay there on the ground moaning in pain, Lombardi showed no sympathy for him whatsoever. As a matter of fact, he continued to yell at him, screaming that he ought to be ashamed of himself for being out of shape. Sonny and I were in the third row, and all I could think was, "Keep yelling, Coach, so I can catch my breath."

Sonny wasn't exempt from Lombardi's wrath. He, like everyone else, feared the man. While rooming with Sonny in the past, I would witness him skipping out after bed check. But not anymore. Lombardi had one of his assistant coaches, Lew Carpenter sit in his station wagon every night until three or four in the morning just in case Jurgensen decided to bolt. Sonny never did, not even once.

One day, early in camp, we had an intrasquad scrimmage. Harland Svare coached the defense while assistant coach Bill Austin coached the offense. Lombardi was up in the press box watching. That day the defense totally dominated the offense. Vince became angrier by the minute. Finally someone yelled from the bleachers, "Heeeeeere he comes!"

Lombardi came stomping down the concrete stairs and stormed over to where the offense was standing. He began to scream and yell at the top of his lungs. He kept it up for quite a while. Just then one of the officials that we had brought in to officiate the game said to Vince, "Coach, you've got two minutes to go."

Lombardi went wild and began screaming at the official. "Two minutes! What the hell do you mean we've got two minutes? I'm running this team, mister, and I'll tell you how much time we've got left!"

No one was exempt from the wrath of Lombardi, not even his wife, Marie.

We were on our way to Philadelphia to play the Eagles and Marie decided to come with us. She usually came to our away games. This particular day we rode the bus from the airport to the Philadelphia Marriott. Vince had dozed off when suddenly we hit a bump in the road that had awakened him. Marie saw that he was awake and asked him, "Vincent, where are we going to eat dinner tonight?"

Poor Marie. Obviously she said the wrong thing and in typical Lombardi manner, Vince yelled, "Lady, let me tell you something. When you travel with this team you get treated like the players! Do you understand? You are going to eat with the team and you're going to eat exactly what they eat! Do you understand?"

Another incident occurred in New Orleans. Vince, Marie, and I were there for a Super Bowl. We were walking down the street when Vince recognized one of his former Packer players, tight end Marv Fleming. By this time Marv had been traded by Green Bay and was now playing for Miami. Fleming had let his hair and sideburns grow real long. All of a sudden Lombardi grabs him and pins him against the wall. He begins screaming at the guy—right there in the street—because his hair was too long!

Lombardi was a definitely a multi-faceted personality. One minute he would be confident and excited, and the next he would get down and depressed. I saw this in him when he began to question his ability to motivate his team. We had just finished our coaching meeting and were headed back to the dorm when Vince turned to me and said, "Sam, I don't think I've got it anymore."

"What are you talking about, Coach?" I said.

"I can't coach anymore, goddamnit. These guys don't know what the hell they're doing. I'm not getting through to them, and they're all over hell on that practice field."

"Coach, that's not true. You're the greatest football coach that's ever been."

"Well, if I'm so goddamned great, why in the hell isn't this team coming together?"

I answered him through experience and perception. "I'll tell you, Coach. When you were in Green Bay and I was with the New York Giants, we knew what you were going to do, but we couldn't stop you. We knew you were going to run off tackle with Jimmy Taylor and we couldn't stop it. We knew you were going to run and sweep with Paul Hornung and we couldn't stop it. And we knew Bart Starr was gong to throw that post pattern to Max McGee and we couldn't stop that either. We couldn't stop you because that team was so fundamentally sound. You could have thrown a football out in the middle of the field and those guys would have known exactly what to do with it.

"Now these Redskins want to perform for you, they really do. But every day you're out there yelling and screaming, and your assistant coaches are yelling and screaming. No one is teaching. These ballplayers want to be exactly like the Packers, and they'll give you everything they've got, but you gotta teach 'em."

Lombardi listened to every word I said then looked at me and proclaimed, "You're right, Sam. Do you know what's happened to me? I've become so damned successful that I forgot what made me successful, and that's teaching people. Tomorrow, we go back to teaching!"

Vince and his coaching staff did go back to teaching the fundamentals of the game and it was the best thing that could have ever happened to the Redskins. But as far as the conditioning went, the rituals remained the same. As a matter of fact, Lombardi had posted a sign in the dressing room that read: "Fatigue makes cowards of us all."

During training camp running back Larry Brown learned the fundamentals of carrying a football—the hard way.

Brown was an eighth round draft choice out of Kansas State and Lombardi liked him from the start. He would tell our running back coach George Dickson to take it easy with Larry because he was such a natural talent. But Larry seemed to have one problem. He couldn't hold on to the ball. If there was one thing that Lombardi hated, it was turnovers. While practicing one day, Vince witnessed Larry fumble and just gave it to him. "Mister, you never fumble the football on me. From now on, Mister, you will eat with this ball, you will sleep with this ball, you will shower with this ball if necessary until you learn how to handle it!"

Poor Larry. He was so embarrassed. The newspapers had pictures of him walking through the cafeteria line with his tray in one hand and a football in the other. But I'll tell you one thing, I can't remember Brown ever fumbling the ball again that year or any other year.

The '69 Season: Saying Good-bye to the Game I Love

By the time the regular season had begun, the Redskins were coming together. We were in the best shape of our lives and optimistic about what the year would hold for us. Hell, why shouldn't we be? We had the greatest coach in the history of the NFL.

As usual there were some personnel changes that year. Bobby Mitchell had retired, but Charley Taylor and Jerry Smith were still catching passes from Sonny. Larry Brown would start at running back and we picked up fullback Charley Harraway off waivers from Cleveland. Our center and All-Pro Len Hauss anchored the offensive line while punter Mike Bragg and place-kicker Curt Knight made up our kicking squad. On defense, I was still the middle linebacker (now 35 years old). I have to admit though that I was surrounded by some outstanding talent in Chris Hanburger on my right and Tom Roussel on my left. Our cornerbacks were Pat Fischer and Mike Bass, and our safeties were Brig Owens and Tom Brown. In the first game Brown injured his shoulder and was replaced by Rickie Harris. We may not have been great, but we definitely felt we were contenders.

We opened up the season against the Saints in New Orleans. Billy Kilmer was the starting quarterback. In the second quarter the score was 10–0, Saints. It was during this game that I flat-out leveled Billy, and he reminds me of it every time he sees me.

We flushed Kilmer out of the pocket and he ran toward the sideline, then came back across the field and was heading to the other side. I was behind him the entire time. Just as he got in front of the Saints' bench, he stepped out of bounds. I hit him with a shot that knocked him straight up in the air and threw him back so far that he landed on a table in front of the team bench. Not only did he break the table, but he bruised his hip in doing so. The Saints team emptied the bench and came after me, as did their owner, John Mecom. I was getting pounded when the officials came over to stop it.

Years later Billy told me that after that hit, he put a reward out on my head. Any player who could knock me out of the game would collect $100 courtesy of Billy Kilmer.

Anyway, late in the fourth quarter we took the lead 26–20 and never looked back. It was the first victory of the Lombardi Era.

The following week we played the Browns in Cleveland. They may have been the defending Eastern Conference champs, but we more than held our own. I know that the Browns won the game 27–24, but I don't remember much more.

In the first half I tried to tackle the Browns running back, Ron Johnson. He ended up kicking me in the head and knocked me out. I returned in the second half. We had intercepted a pass and I was looking for a player to block. Along came 265-pound offensive tackle Monte Clark. Clark was known for his holding, so now it was time for a little revenge. There was just one problem. He ended up hitting me first and the lights went out a second time.

I came to on the sidelines to the sight of Dr. Resta. He looked into my eyes and said, "Sam, you better start thinking about that other career."

The following week we played the 49ers in San Francisco. The game ended in a 17–17 tie, but in our home opener at Robert F. Kennedy Memorial Stadium (formally District of Columbia Stadium) we beat St. Louis 33–17. Our win streak continued as we beat the Giants 20–14 and the Steelers 14–7. But in the third quarter of the Pittsburgh game I got knocked out, but was able to return and help hold on to the lead with only minutes to go.

The Steelers were driving, threatening to tie the game, when I was sent in. On third down, defensive back, Bob Wade (who later went on to coach basketball at the University of Maryland), knocked away a pass from Terry Hanratty. And on fourth down he tackled Earl Gros at the 5 with an assist from me, and we won the game.

At the end of the game Lombardi smiled and said through his excitement, "You people are going to give me a heart attack."

We were now 4-1-1 and the city of Washington was elated. That is, until the Colts came to town.

In that game we gained 357 yards on offense, but we had a punt blocked, numerous interceptions and fumbles, and 89 yards in penalties. Baltimore humiliated the Redskins by a score of 41–17.

In Week 8 we ended up with a heartbreaking 28–28 tie with the Eagles. The decision came from two bad officiating calls. With less than two minutes to play in the game Washington was up 28–21. The Eagles had a fourth-and-25 at our 42. Philly quarterback Norm Snead dropped back and threw deep for Ben Hawkins. Mike Bass was on Hawkins the entire time. Both went up for the ball, but the ball fell incomplete. It was basically an uncatchable pass, but the official threw his flag and Bass got nailed for pass interference. The Eagles ended up getting the ball on the 1 and on the next play they scored. Lombardi was beside himself.

With less than a minute left in the game, the Redskins got the ball back. Sonny let one go to Charley Taylor who was downfield and just as he was about to make the catch he was smacked by both Irv Cross and Joe Scarpati. It was obviously pass interference, but just as the official was about to reach for his flag, he stopped. He never threw it! If he had, or if Charley had caught the pass we would have had the ball at the Eagle 35 with enough time to try for a field goal. Instead, we ended up punting and an eventual tie.

Lombardi was livid. He was all over the officials. He was so enraged that he followed them into their dressing room and screamed at them through the door. After that he came to our locker room and screamed at us.

Vince had calmed down by Tuesday's press conference. He also told them a story about a discovery regarding Larry Brown. "While watching game films I noticed that Larry wasn't getting off the ball right away. When the quarterback tells the team he wants the ball snapped on the count of three, when you hear three, you move. That gives the offense an instant of advantage because you know what the count is and the defense doesn't. Now, everyone was moving at the snap, but Larry was just a bit late.

"I realized that something was wrong and confronted Larry with the problem. I told him, 'Mister, you're not getting off the ball. What's the matter with you, can't you hear?'

"Larry looked at me and said, 'No sir, I'm deaf in one ear.' What I didn't know was that Larry had been having trouble hearing the snap count, particularly with big crowds in the stadium. This forced him to wait until he saw movement before he left his position. Tim Temerario, our team's director of player personnel, came up with the idea of building a hearing aid into Larry's helmet, and I thought it was worth a try. They got it done, and one day in the locker room, I had Larry walk to the other side of the room and put his helmet on while I walked over to the other. I asked him if he could hear me. He replied, 'Coach, I never did have any trouble hearing you!'"

Over the next three weeks we lost to both the Cowboys and Rams, but beat the Falcons. Week 12 saw us pitted once more against the Eagles, but this time revenge would be sweet. We routed them 34–29 and Brown and his hearing aid gained 138 yards. We were now 6–4–2. We were guaranteed a .500 season, but Lombardi wanted a winning season. In his 15 years as an assistant coach and head coach with the NFL, Vince never had a losing season. On the other hand, the Redskins hadn't finished over .500 since 1955.

Next up were the Saints. We beat them 17–14 and were assured of a winning season. Our final game was against the Cowboys. We lost 20–10 but there was a great feeling of satisfaction at what this team had accomplished.

The Dallas game was also the final game of my professional football career as a player. I knew I would never play again, but was thankful to Lombardi for one last opportunity. I can remember one day late in the '69 season when we were reviewing game film and all of a sudden Lombardi yelled out, "Who the hell is No. 70? We've got to replace him!"

"Hey, wait a minute, Coach. That's me," I said.

"Oh, I didn't realize that was you, Sam."

Of course he knew it was me, but there was no apology. That was just his way of letting me know that it was time to hang 'em up. I knew it, too.

Late in the season we had begun to train Marlin McKeever to play the middle linebacker position and by the end of the year, I wasn't playing very much. Nearing the end of the Dallas game, I was standing on the sidelines when my friend Harland came up to me and did the nicest thing that any coach has ever done for me. "Sam, you're too great a player to go out standing on the sideline. Why don't you just go in there and finish up the game."

There's not much I can say about what happened during those few, short series, but what I can tell you is that right to the end, I was still the man in the middle.

FOURTH QUARTER
LIFE AFTER FOOTBALL

Tackling Politics

With my playing days behind me, it was time to look toward the future. I wanted to become a coach in the NFL and was prepared to take whatever steps necessary to begin at the assistant coaching level.

I had already been working with John Didion, Harold McLinton, and Tom Roussel—the Redskins' young linebackers—and was planning to be a full-time assistant in 1970 under Lombardi. Immediately following the end of the '69 season, we began getting ready for 1970. We reviewed film, scouted college players in the postseason all-star games, and began going over team personnel lists to see who would be available in the fall.

While this was all going on, I received a call from Wesley Bagby, a political science professor at West Virginia University. He had followed my career since my West Virginia days as a Mountaineer up until my retirement. He was interested to know if I would be interested in running against Senator Robert Byrd—then the most powerful politician in the state. Bagby was the head of a liberal group with over 1,000 members called the Coalition for Alternatives to Senator Byrd. They had chosen me to run. To say that I was flattered would have been an understatement.

I was always fascinated by politics. As a matter of fact I had campaigned for John F. Kennedy in 1960 in the West Virginia primary. I can remember the first time I met Kennedy. My old friend, John Manchin, asked me if I might introduce Kennedy at a function back home in Farmington. I told him I would be proud to do so.

A few days later I met with the Kennedy entourage and sat in the back of the car with the candidate. This was the first time I had met the man and his intelligence and knowledge of politics and people was incredible. He turned to me and said, "Sam, these are your people. You were born and raised here. You understand them. What do you think I ought to talk about?"

At the time, Kennedy's religious preference had become a big issue. There had never been a Catholic president voted into office. I shared my thoughts with him. "Senator Kennedy, when my dad found out I was going to introduce you today, he asked me why I'd want to do a thing like that. I told him I thought you were a good man and that you could help the people of West

Virginia. My dad said to me, 'Son, I don't want the Pope running the country.' That rang a bell in my head. Here was a typical West Virginian, a coal miner, and that's what was on his mind. Senator, I really do believe these people will think a whole lot more of you if you talk about being Catholic and what that means. It's like baseball. If a guy's going to throw you a fastball, be set to hit the fastball. Don't be guessing. Don't be wondering. Just be truthful with them."

That day he gave an outstanding speech which included what we had discussed on the way into town. "I want to tell you good people that when I joined the service of our country, no one asked me if I was a Catholic, a Protestant, or a Jew because I was there to fight a war."

This was all off the cuff. He held the audience's attention in the palm of his hand. The man was absolutely amazing. We traveled throughout the state and Kennedy gave that same speech. He went on to win the primary and beat out Hubert Humphrey to win the nomination. I'm not going to say that our conversation was directly responsible for him winning the presidency, but it sure didn't hurt him in West Virginia.

I campaigned all over the state for Kennedy and got to know Bobby and Ethel and Ted. The family was incredible. One day as I was campaigning with Teddy, I realized that here is a guy from one of the richest families in America and I'm the one who is always buying the coffee and sandwiches. I finally said to Teddy, "This has got to stop. I don't have this kind of money."

He laughed and said, "Well, Sam, rich people never carry any money with them."

I quickly responded with, "Then rich people are going to go hungry, because I've bought you your last sandwich."

The last time I saw JFK was at the College Football Hall of Fame dinner in New York. I attended the event with a little-known, local radio announcer by the name of Howard Cosell. The President was up on the dais when Howard told me to go up and say hello to him. "He knows you worked for him in 1960 so just walk up and renew old acquaintances."

Even back then, Howard was aggressive.

I worked my way toward the president but was stopped by Secret Service. One of the guys recognized me, but because I didn't have an identification badge, I wasn't allowed up. I saw Bill Shea—the man who Shea Stadium was named after—and asked him if I could borrow his pin so I could go up and talk to Kennedy. He gave it to me and I got through security. I walked up to the President and right away he stood up and shook my hand. He was wondering what had taken me so long to get there. He had been expecting me.

We talked for 15 minutes and he invited me to the White House. When I came back down from the podium, one of the Secret Service men stopped me and said, "You know, my boss doesn't stand up and talk to anyone for that long. You really must be a good friend."

I'd like to think that's true. It would be the last time I would ever see John Kennedy alive.

Ever since my experience with the Kennedys, politics continued to intrigue me. I've always considered it an honor to call West Virginia home, but as I researched the senate race, it became clear that Senator Byrd was simply too powerful. I decided to talk with John Manchin and other friends of mine about running for Congress in the First Congressional District. They agreed that I should.

After the season, I spoke to Lombardi about my plans. Being the patriot that he was, he was extremely excited about my running and gave me his blessing. During my campaign, he made appearances for me in Washington to help raise funds. He told me that if things didn't go as planned that I could come back and be an assistant coach for him.

My opponent was the 61-year-old incumbent Robert H. Mollohan. He had served in Congress in the early 1950s and later went on to become an executive with the United Mine Workers. In my opinion, he was nothing more than an inept congressman who never did a damned thing for the district. Throughout the years I'd heard many accounts of his political wheeling and dealing. In the '40s it was alleged that he had used his influence to acquire leases from the state for a coal company to mine coal on state-owned school property. There were canceled checks made out personally to Mollohan from the coal company. It was also alleged that the coal company set him up with a free car and house. That information was released when he ran for governor in 1956. The reason he was never prosecuted was because the local district attorney felt that the statute of limitations had expired. In my opinion, regardless how you look at it, Bob Mollohan was a corrupt politician.

The political underhandedness began as soon as I announced my candidacy. I wanted to make the announcement at my old high school in Farmington, but the Marion County superintendent of schools told me I couldn't. I knew right then and there who was pulling all the strings.

I decided to visit Mr. Dodrill, the principal of the high school, and took John Manchin along with me. Needless to say, we were both angry about the situation.

When we arrived at the school, John immediately started yelling at Dodrill. "Who the hell do you think paid for this carpet on the floor? I did, that's who!"

I decided to tone it down a little when addressing the principal. "Mr. Dodrill, I get a lump in my throat whenever I walk into this school. I love this place, and neither you nor any other cheap politician is going to stop me from making my announcement here. If you intend to stop me, you had better call out the National Guard, because that's what it will take."

On February 7, I announced my candidacy to run for Congress at Farmington High School. All the major networks and reports were there. Over the next three months I covered 220 miles from north to south. John Manchin, his son Joe Manchin, and a childhood friend of mine, Buck Basile, rode out the campaign trail with me. Before that three-month crusade had ended I had worn out two pairs of shoes, a couple of sets of tires and my own voice. But my efforts were futile because Mollohan's political machine would not allow anyone to come between them and their incumbent.

The mudslinging and rumors were horrific! I was called a carpetbagger even though I owned a house in the district in Rock Lake; called a traitor by the Democratic party because I had met with my friend Arch Moore, the then-Republican governor of the state, to get his opinion on my political options before running; and that I was divorcing my wife and having an affair with Ethel Kennedy.

Politics in the state of West Virginia were controlled by the UMW, the Teamsters, and the AFL-CIO. They had total control of the numbers rackets and pinball machines, then would turn around and donate money to the churches, the Little Leagues, and the local charities in order to stay in control. Their method was effective, but I wasn't about to play by their rules.

I spoke to one of the high-ranking officials of the Teamsters union about getting their support. His response was, "Sam, I'm going to tell you the truth. I've known you since you were a little boy. I've admired you and followed you through your entire football career, and there's no doubt in my mind you would make a great congressman. But that's not what we want. We have what we want in Bob Mollohan. When we say jump, he jumps. You've never done that, and you never will. You've made it tough for me because I have to work like hell to make sure you don't get elected. I don't like it, but I have to do it."

While campaigning in downtown Mannington, I began speaking with the chief of police. It was quite obvious that he didn't want to hear what I had to say when he interrupted me. "Sam, I can't back you. At night, I work at the drive-in theater. I run the projector. My boss there is a strong Mollohan man. If I back you, I lose that job."

I countered with, "When you step in that voting booth, buddy, nobody knows how you'll vote. Not even your boss at the theater."

This is what I was up against. My entire platform was to prove that Mollohan had not done one thing for his district. Part of my campaign speeches had to do with the fact that West Virginia had more people killed in wars based on percentage of population than any other state in the union, and yet we had less defense spending than any other state. People started to take notice.

One day I got a call from one of my neighbors in Alexandria, Virginia. He worked for the Navy Department and told me that the navy was gong to come to West Virginia to start planning a helicopter plant in Clarksburg. He told me that my opponent felt the pressure and was forced to do something about the defense spending in West Virginia. I knew that I had gotten to Mollohan, and at this point I really felt that he would have to fight for each and every vote. Then reality set in.

I attended a sports banquet at Fairmont State College with my little brother John, who had played on the school's football team. That season he kicked a field goal that won the national small college championship for the school. Not only did they not introduce me, they didn't even acknowledge my brother! L.O. Bickle, a local businessman who was one of the school's big boosters and the master of ceremonies that night, came up to me after the dinner and said, "I'm sure you understand, Sam."

I squeezed his hand so hard he almost had tears in his eyes. "I will never understand how one West Virginian can treat another like this. You didn't have to acknowledge my presence, but you also short-changed my brother, and I'm going to get even. Someday, I'll pay you back for this because you embarrassed my family and me."

The underhandedness and the blackballing continued throughout the media and even with friends of mine. By this point, I knew it was all over.

I ended up losing to Mollohan by a margin of two to one. I even lost in my hometown of Farmington, and that really hurt. The experience was traumatic and to this day it leaves a bitter taste in my mouth.

The Passing of a Legend

A few weeks after I rejoined Lombardi and the Redskins staff, I happened to pass Vince in the hall. He had a habit of walking around with his head down and his hands behind his back, but this particular day he didn't look well. I asked him if he was feeling okay.

"I think I have the flu, Sam."

I mentioned to him that he should see our team physician, Dr. Resta.

"I think you're right. I better do that. I'm not feeling well at all."

He was admitted to Georgetown University Hospital and a battery of tests were run. It was discovered that he had colon cancer. Lombardi had always refused to have physical examinations and was dead set against proctology exams. It cost him his life.

Immediately the doctors removed a section of his colon. Soon after that, I went to visit him in the hospital. He had difficulty talking, but he truly believed that he could beat the disease. We talked about the good ol' days with the Giants where he'd always wanted to return as a coach. "The timing was just never right, but I have no regrets."

The next time I saw Lombardi was when we were scrimmaging against the Colts in Baltimore. He had been out of the hospital for a couple of weeks, but he looked extremely weak and frail. He had lost about 40 pounds and his voice was a whisper.

Vince gathered the team around him and specifically directed his comments to the younger players that he had drafted that spring. "You are my people. I've selected you. You're going to wear this uniform with pride. You're now a member of the Washington Redskins, and there's a lot of responsibility that goes along with that. Don't you ever forget it."

It was an extremely moving experience that night for everyone in that room. It would be the last time I ever saw Vince Lombardi alive.

The following day he was readmitted to Georgetown Hospital for a second operation. On September 3, 1970, Vince Lombardi died. His passing was mourned all over America.

Edward Bennett Williams had this to say at Lombardi's eulogy: "He had a covenant with greatness. He was committed to excellence in everything he attempted. Our country has lost one of its great men. The world of sport has lost its first citizen. The Redskins have lost their leader. I personally have lost a friend."

What made the man so great? He not only had the infinite desire to excel, but he knew how to get it out of his player. He knew how to sell us on his game plan: "We will win if we do this, this, and this." And everyone always believed him. He was a smart coach who believed in fundamentals. He would always say, "I don't care what you do offensively. You can go in motion put up an I-formation use a triple-flanker set, but the team that blocks the hardest and tackles the hardest is going to win this game."

In 1969 Lombardi had taken the Redskins and literally willed them to a winning season. I honestly believe that if he had lived Washington would have gone on to be a dominant football team for as long as Lombardi was there.

But there was one decision that Vince made from his hospital bed in August when he believed that he would beat the cancer and rejoin the team. He appointed his No. 1 assistant (both in Green Bay and Washington), Bill Austin, as the interim coach of the '70 Redskins.

Unfortunately Lombardi died two weeks prior to the start of the regular season and Austin, I, and the rest of the staff stayed on for the remainder of the year.

As an assistant coach, Austin did a great job, but as head coach, well, that's another story. He was difficult to work with and extremely negative. The players weren't exactly elated to work with him. The rest of our staff was excellent. We had Mike McCormack, who later became a Hall of Fame member and general manager of the Seattle Seahawks franchise; Don Doll; Lew Carpenter; George Dickson; and Harland Svare.

As far as the team went, our offense was pretty damned good, but our defense couldn't stop anyone. They were so pathetic that when we played the Lions in our fourth game of the season, Dickson came into our coaches' meeting yelling, "There's no way we can win this game! Absolutely no way!"

Even though the Lions had beaten the Bears on *Monday Night Football*—and I have to admit that they did look awesome, I had never in my life heard a coach say that. In my mind, I felt that there was always a way to win. And we did win! We changed our defense and beat the Lions 31–10.

As the season wore on, our defense continued to deteriorate. It got so bad that Austin would come into our defensive meetings and sarcastically say to his staff, "Well, how are you guys going to screw up this week?"

The offense had talent in guys like Charley Taylor, Sonny, Larry Brown, and Jerry Smith. The defense had nothing. Each week became more difficult than the other as we found ourselves having to come up with something different that would outsmart our opponents.

We were about to play the Cowboys when Austin started raggin' on us again. We knew that Dallas would be a tough opponent, but his bitchin' and complaining had just gotten to me. "You know, Austin, you were a jerk in high school, a jerk in college, you were a jerk when we played together in New York, and you'll be a jerk all your life! So let's see just how good of a coach you are. I'll tell you what. We'll switch this week. Let us coach your offense and you coach the defense, and we'll see how damned great you are."

Normally, those type of remarks were enough to get anyone fired, but I knew that we would all be gone come the end of the season and Bennett would hire a whole new staff complete with a high-caliber coach.

Bill stormed out of the room and Harland laid into me. I wasn't about to take it from him either. "I'm tired of people picking on us with the kind of players that we have! I'm not about to sit here and take that. I've never in my life pulled against my own team, but it wouldn't bother me a bit if the Cowboys shut that offense out!"

And that's exactly what happened. Cowboys 34, Redskins 0.

Near the end of the season, Harland and I were driving to practice from Alexandria when I asked him if he had another job lined up after the season had ended.

"What are you talking about, Sam? Just because you don't get along with Austin doesn't mean that I don't."

"Harland," I said, "Bill is history. He won't have a job here next year."

"Well, I think he can do the job," said Harland.

"He won't have a chance to do the job. Just look at Ed Williams' track record. He fired McPeak and brought in a big name: Otto Graham. He fired Graham and he brought in a big name: Vince Lombardi. This team is going nowhere and I guarantee you it's over for all of us."

"We'll see," said Harland.

And we did.

Not long after the season ended, Williams met with Austin and told him he was fired. When Bill gave us the news, I took it upon myself to clean out all the offices. I took all the film—both offensive and defensive—the playbooks, and the overlays for the slide projectors that diagrammed all the plays and patterns. I basically took everything that had to do with our staff and loaded it up in my car. I wasn't stealing it; I just wanted the work that we had created to stay with us. Anyone who wanted it would have to come to my home in Alexandria to get it.

On January 6, 1971, Williams hired George Allen as his new head coach. George had come over from the Los Angeles Rams, and he took the time to interview each and every one of us who were on Austin's staff. When he interviewed me, I knew he had no intention whatsoever of hiring me as the team's linebacker coach. He, himself, coached the linebackers. He just wanted to pick everyone's brain. When he was finished, he went ahead and hired his own staff. Typical Allen style.

The Marriott Experience

By this time, I began to have doubts as to whether or not I wanted my career in football to continue. I called around the league to see what was available, but nothing seemed to pan out. By February I was still out of work. I'd received a few offers from friends, but nothing caught my interest. Then it hit me.

One day I was driving down River Road in Washington and noticed a sign that read "Marriott Corporate Headquarters." That's when the light bulb began to flicker in my head. I was a stockholder in Marriott and had read that its biggest problem was filling the hotels on weekends. That gave me another idea.

When I played with the Giants, we always flew on United. United would assign a company rep to the team, which they did for many of the NFL clubs. The rep was responsible for all the details, and the service was great. Each time we traveled we had the same pilots and the same crew. The buses were always on time and our bags were always waiting for us. There was never a holdup at the airport or the hotel.

I came up with the idea to incorporate United's program to the Marriott hotel industry for sports teams. With all my marketing experience with Philip Morris and J.P. Stevens, I developed a proposal to have college and professional football teams stay at the Marriott hotels on the weekends when they played their games. My only problem was that I didn't know anyone in the corporation. I decided to ask the Redskins' publicity man, Joe Blair, for help. He told me that Bill Marriott, the son of founder J.W. Marriott, was now in charge of the hotel chain and was also a big Redskins fan. Joe thought it would be in my best interest to give him a call. So I did.

When I called Bill Marriott's office, his secretary, Mary Harne, answered the phone. He was out of the office at the time so I left my name with Mary and asked her to have Mr. Marriott call me. Just then she asked, "Are you the Sam Huff who played for the Redskins?"

"Yes, Ma'am."

"I can't believe it, Mr. Huff. I'm a very big Redskins fan. Don't worry, he'll get the message."

To this day I credit Mary for getting me in to see Bill.

The following week I met with Bill Marriott. I presented him with my proposal and he was very excited about it. So excited that he picked up the phone and called Jim Durbin, the head of the hotel division, and said, "Sam Huff's in here and he's got a plan to help us with these weekend problems. I want you to hire him."

The next day I met with Durbin. I told him that I needed a secretary, an office, a company car, and $30,000 a year. He told me I would be working with a guy by the name of Al LeFaivre who would train and educate me about the hotel business, and instead of $30,000 a year I would be making $35,000 a year.

LeFaivre didn't know football and I didn't know the hotel business. I told him I'd teach him about the game if he would teach me about the business, but things didn't quite work out that way. He refused to give me an office or a secretary. Instead, he supplied me with a desk and a telephone, and the use of his secretary.

Al did little to train me, so I decided to do it on my own. I called Frank Gifford and he suggested that I speak with the *Monday Night Football* crew about staying at the various Marriott hotels. The crews would arrive on Thursday to set up, and they would number anywhere from 45 to 50 people. This was exactly what Bill Marriott was looking for. I not only sealed the deal with the pros, but also with the colleges. In 1987 alone we accumulated 40 to 50 million dollars in revenue just from sports-related business.

When we moved our headquarters to Bethesda, we didn't have a very big parking lot. With land being so expensive, the parking lot was reserved solely for corporate vice presidents. Everyone else had to fend for themselves. I constantly asked Bill for my own parking space, but he was adamant about his ruling. One day after I had been elected into the Pro Football Hall of Fame, the company honored me. Bill gave a speech and then told the crowd that he had decided to modify the company rules a bit. "The only people who will get their own parking spaces are corporate vice presidents, and members of the Pro Football Hall of Fame."

I began my Marriott career as a salesman, worked my way up to Director of Sports Marketing and ended as Vice President of the company. The corporation and I built a great relationship over the 27 years that I worked for them.

Radio Days and Broadcasting the Redskins

I began my career in radio in Washington while I was still playing ball. I conducted locker-room shows for WMAL radio. After the '67 season I did some sports shows for ABC radio in New York that also included a scoreboard show. Not only was the experience good training, but ABC even hired a speech coach to help me with my diction and pronunciation.

While I was still working for J.P. Stevens I was offered a job as a sportscaster with the ABC affiliate in New York. I later found out that the job was to be one of the original *Monday Night Football* team.

After Austin and the rest of us were dismissed, WNEW in New York hired me as the color man for the Giants games. A lot had changed with the Giants organization. Allie Sherman had been fired and replaced by my teammate Alex Webster. It was also at this time that Wellington Mara and I resolved our differences. In fact, Wellington encouraged me to take the position.

I worked with an old veteran of broadcasting by the name of Marty Glickman and a guy named Chip Cipolla, who was a popular local sportscaster. The problem with Cipolla was that he was always taking cheap shots at the Giants. I was the one who was sent to the locker room to do the postgame show, because if Cipolla had gone down there the players might have killed him.

Cipolla and I never did hit it off and we had some major arguments on the air. I remember one time on our halftime show when we were supposed to interview Neil Armstrong. While on the air, Cipolla actually forgot Armstrong's name. Marty Glickman had been listening and became so angry that he ripped off his headset and threw it against the wall.

Marv Albert, who was then the voice of the New York Knicks and the New York Rangers, replaced Glickman as the play-by-play man in 1973. He was a great guy to work with and we had a great year together. That job allowed me to keep my hand in the game, and for me that was always the best part.

The most difficult part of the job was the traveling. Between the preseason and regular season, I had to travel 20 weekends a year, and I was still living in Virginia. It took its toll on me, and in 1974 Andy Ockershausen asked me to join WMAL radio in Washington. I took the job.

I worked with several different play-by-play guys over the first couple of years. In the mid-1970s Sonny Jurgensen left CBS and joined us in the booth. It was Sonny and I and a guy by the name of Frank Herzog, who was the best damned play-by-play man in the business. We were together for years. Sonny would get on me, I would get on Sonny, and Frank would keep it all together.

With both Sonny and I former Redskins players, you know that the broadcast is biased. I am the first to admit that, and besides our listeners are Redskins fans. But we do respect the opposing team and have no trouble criticizing Washington when they don't get the job done. I remember Sonny getting all over Joe Theismann and later on Jay Schroeder in 1987.

It was never a mystery to anyone that Jurgensen and Theismann didn't get along. Sonny and Billy Kilmer both loathed Joe and his running off at the mouth when he joined the team in 1974.

In 2005 Larry Michael took over Frank Herzog's seat and became our referee. I always used to say, "Defense wins championships. Everybody knows that." Sonny would always say, "People pay to see the offense."

Whatever the case, I've kept to one simple philosophy in broadcasting a football game. If I can make all of our listeners understand the game, then I've done my job.

The day I fail to do that, they can come and throw me out of the booth.

The Hall Of Fame

The day I was inducted into the Pro Football Hall of Fame in Canton, Ohio, was one of the greatest days of my life. But there were times when I began to doubt it would ever happen.

Part of the criteria to be selected requires that you have been out of the game for a minimum of five years. But it wasn't until 13 years after I retired from playing, 1982, that I finally was voted in.

I wouldn't have minded it as much if there were no other middle linebackers from my era already in the Hall, but that was not the case. Bill George, Dick Butkus, and Ray Nitschke got in, all in the first year of their eligibility!

I began to question myself—my skill and talent as a player. But, hell, I played in six championship games, played on a world championship team, and probably blocked more kicks than any man in the history of the game. I had 30 career interceptions—more than any linebacker at that time—was on the cover of *Time Magazine*, and Walter Cronkite narrated my story on national television. I was decent to the media, never wore white shoes, never, ever wore my hair long or shot off my mouth—well, I guess that last one is debatable—but I just didn't understand it!

There was no question in my mind that many of the voters still remembered my battles with Jim Brown and Jimmy Taylor. I'm sure the guys who voted in Cleveland and Green Bay were not exactly hot on me getting in. There was a lot of resentment toward me because I played for a high-profile team that just happened to be located in the media capital of the world.

When I attended the 1982 Super Bowl I was mentally ready for another frustrating week. On top of it all, the game was held that year in Pontiac, Michigan, where the temperature never went higher than the teens. Of course, this forced everyone to spend most of their time in the hotel lobbies. For me, personally, that made the anticipation of the vote that much more crucial.

I ran into Ray Nitschke on the day of the voting. He said, "Sam, you deserve to be in the Hall of Fame, and I think this is the year you're going to make it. I can feel it."

It was nice to hear Ray say that, but it didn't ease the knot in my stomach.

On the morning of the vote, Mary and I ran into the executive director of the Hall of Fame, Pete Elliott. He had just left the meeting and he smiled when he saw us. "You made it, Sam!"

My mind had trouble making sense of the words. Once it hit me, I began to cry, as did Mary. We were both standing in the lobby with tears streaming down our faces. The hardest part of all was that I couldn't tell anyone. The official announcement wouldn't be made until the following week at the Pro Bowl. Do you know how hard it was for me to keep it a secret? And for an entire week! In today's NFL, the voting takes place the Saturday before the Super Bowl and the winners are announced that same day. The new class is introduced at the Super Bowl.

The Class of 1982 would be inducted in August. There were only four inductees that year: George Musso, Merlin Olsen, Doug Atkins, and I. My presenter was Tom Landry. Tom was so kind to me. He left training camp at Thousand Oaks, California, to fly to Ohio for the ceremony. As part of his introductory speech, Tom said, "I never had any trouble with Sam because any time he started to goof off, I would give him the choice of getting the job done for the Giants or going back to the coal mines of West Virginia. It was amazing how quickly he got his act together.

"When the decision was made to move Sam to middle linebacker, I wasn't sure he could make the transition. However, it wasn't long before I realized that his dedication and competitive attitude were ideally suited for the position. It wasn't long before we realized that Sam was something special."

Then it was my turn to speak. To tell you the truth, I can't really remember what I said, but I do remember looking at the crowd and seeing my entire family before me. Your mind is filled with so many thoughts and emotions. I've seen many guys get choked up while giving their speech. Luckily I was able to contain myself, but there were times when I thought I would lose it. I thought of my parents and how much they had sacrificed for me, about Ray Kelly and Art Lewis and how proud they would have been, about Landry and Lombardi and all my teammates: Kat and Gifford, Little Mo and Rosey, Yat and Andy, and my roommates, Don Chandler and Sonny.

That Hall of Fame ring is one of my most prized possessions and every time I look at it I realize how fortunate I have been.

Just as a sidebar…

On Saturday, February 5, the Hall of Fame Class of 2011 was announced. I was extremely excited and very proud to hear that Chris Hanburger was named as one of seven inductees. Chris was drafted in 1965 by the Redskins and played outside linebacker with me. I later went on to coach him, and he developed into one fine player. No. 55 was also the linebacker who helped the

Washington Redskins reach their first Super Bowl in 1972, as a key member of former coach George Allen's Over the Hill Gang.

My Life Today...

On any given day you will find me on my 22-acre ranch in Middleburg, Virginia—the middle of horse country. The home I live in, I designed myself. I can remember as a kid having to share a bed with my brother, Don. I'd always dreamed of one day owning a house like this, and now my dream has come true.

Since I was a child listening to Roy Rogers and Gene Autry on the radio, I have been fascinated with horses. In 1983 I visited a stud farm in Lexington, Kentucky, and fell in love with a thoroughbred. I bought a third of it for $15,000. Since then, I've bought shares in many other horses. My partner in the horse business is a woman who loves horses as much as I do. Her name is Carol Holden and she has been there for me through thick and thin. She is a wonderful person and keeps me grounded. Together we have been working on upgrading racing in West Virginia. In 1987 we hosted the West Virginia Breeders Classic. It was the first $100,000 horse race in the history of the state. It has now become an annual event.

I consider myself to have led a wonderful life, but I have worked extremely hard for everything that I have ever achieved. I grew up in a coal mining camp and knew right from the start that this was not how I was going to spend the rest of my life. I wanted something far better. That something was a college education and the sport of football. It made me the man I am today, and I am grateful for the opportunities it has afforded me.

Brothers of the Redskins' Legacy— Keepers of the Flame

In 1964 both Sonny and I came to Redskins unwillingly, but looking back— nearly 50 years later, neither one of us would change a thing. After all, it has been, and continues to be, an amazing journey.

By 1959 I had already been with the Giants for four years. That was also the year that I became the first pro player to appear on the cover of *Time Magazine*. In 1960 I became the subject of a television special hosted by Walter Cronkite titled "The Violent World of Sam Huff." And it was also in 1960 that I first heard the name Sonny Jurgensen. Sonny was the backup to Philly's starting quarterback, Norm Van Brocklin.

Tom Landry gave a scouting report when we were going to play the Philadelphia Eagles and he said, "I don't want you to hit Norm Van Brocklin, because if you hurt him Sonny Jurgensen is going to come in. And let me tell you now you don't want to play against Jurgensen, because he can really throw that football."

Van Brocklin retired in 1961 and Sonny immediately took over. In his first year as a starter he was voted an All-Pro, setting the NFL season record for passing yards and tying the record for touchdowns. The Eagles finished the season 10–4, but the aging team had reached its pinnacle of success.

Over the next two years, Sonny continued to be the strength of Philadelphia, but his teammates became riddled with injuries and declined with age. The Eagles were about to enter a decade-long freefall, and by the end of 1963 the Giants were faced with a parallel fate.

As both the Giants and Eagles prepared to rebuild, no one was safe from the trading block. Little did Sonny or I know that we were about to be blindsided!

At the end of the 1963 season, I led New York to their sixth championship game in eight years. I was on top of the world, but behind the scenes, a silent deterioration of the team was spreading.

It began in 1959 when Lombardi went to Green Bay and continued when Landry set out to build an expansion team in Dallas called the Cowboys.

Back in 1961 offensive coordinator Allie Sherman became the head coach and single-handedly began to dismantle the defense. One by one he traded us off, and in '64 it was my turn.

Luckily for me, my future best friend was on the same train to report to the Redskins training camp.

In Sonny's case, the Eagles had won only two games in 1963 and a new coaching staff was put into place. Jurgensen had missed most of the season due to injury and was looking forward to turning things around in 1964.

On April Fool's Day, new head coach Joe Kuharich promised Sonny that opportunity, but his dreams were short lived. He would soon come to realize that the NFL breaks promises as easily as arm tackles. Before he knew it, Sonny was on his way to the Redskins.

Sonny had gone to the Eagles' office to meet with Joe Kuharich and had a very productive meeting. They talked about what they wanted to do and how they were going to go about it. Sonny then left to go to lunch. While at lunch some guy walked into the restaurant to tell Sonny that he had just been traded to Washington. He thought he was joking because it was April Fool's Day. Sonny was in shock. He could not believe that the Eagles had done that to him.

By the time Jurgensen reported to Washington and signed with head coach Bill McPeak, the shock had worn off and he embraced the chance to start fresh. If you had seen me at my press conference, you would have thought the same thing. I may have been smiling on the outside, but underneath that façade of confidence, I was scared to death that I was losing it all.

When Sonny and I came to Washington, the Redskins were a laughing stock. But we would help to change that. In reality, the game of football would have pit us against each other as gridiron enemies—a quarterback and a linebacker—but we went on to become team leaders, roommates, and best friends.

Sonny and I agreed that he would run the offense and I would run the defense. We blended. It was a team that needed leadership, and it was up to us to provide the leadership.

Unfortunately for us, the Redskins season began with four straight losses, one of which— the Giants—I took very personally. I wanted so badly to stick it to Sherman, but the game turned out to be a disaster.

I will never forget that game. We were winning and the Giants ran a handoff, and the quarterback missed the handoff. He staggered into the end zone on a busted play to beat us. Sonny and I had tears in our eyes walking to the locker room at Yankee Stadium. It was a game I didn't want to lose.

Our 0–4 season looked as though it was unsalvageable; that is, until Sonny and his former Philadelphia team were reunited. This time the revenge would be especially sweet, and Washington would begin their reign in the win column. Sonny wanted to show his old team what a mistake it was to trade him and his new team what it felt like to win.

After Sonny had been traded, like me, it was always a special game for him.

We ended up winning 6 of our last 10 games of the '64 season. Sonny was unstoppable, and along with the rest of our explosive offense, we became one of the NFL's most dominant teams.

Sonny had a great arm and could throw the ball. He also had a great mind. He was so well prepared that when the coaches called a play that he didn't like, he just called his own. I don't think that any safety could read him because he had a windmill release and you didn't know where that ball was coming out in that arch. I have yet to see a quarterback who can throw the ball like Sonny did. He could throw the ball better than anybody I had ever seen. He could put that thing right where he wanted to put it.

Our defense wasn't too bad either.

My impact on opponents was immediate. I always made sure that they felt the hit and never let go of my killer instinct. I used to put my head down and stick it to my opponent, telling him that I was going to knock him into the next row of seats. I always had a comment for the other team after every play. "Let's see what you got!" That's how I played the game—all-out, all the time.

Throughout the mid-'60s, Sonny and I inspired a team and a fan base that sparked a home sellout streak that has yet to be broken. We changed the attitude of the Redskins, we changed the attitude of everybody who went to RFK Stadium, and we changed the entire attitude of sports in Washington D.C. To play in the nation's capital was special.

The Redskins had finally gained respectability. Sonny and I were on a roll, but in week six of the '67 season, I severely injured my ankle and my streak of 150 consecutive games played had come to an end. I was unable to return to play until late in the year. It was then that I had decided that it was time to retire.

But I came back in '69 as a player/coach under new head coach Vince Lombardi. With both Sonny and me leading the team, Washington set the stage for its most successful season in more than a decade. We finished with a 7–5–2 record. The franchise had been revived and the future was filled with promise. Sadly enough, fate didn't see it the same way.

Coach Lombardi was diagnosed with colon cancer, and died shortly thereafter. To say that we were all crushed by the loss of Lombardi would be an understatement, but Sonny and me had now shared an even stronger bond. Lombardi not only changed my life, but he had now changed Sonny's as well.

Sonny was so thankful to have been given the opportunity to play for Lombardi. The way Coach lived and his strong belief in winning made losing not an option. He thought the world of Sonny Jurgensen. It was a wonderful partnership.

In 1970 I coached the linebackers, but when George Allen arrived in 1971, I was released. Little did I know that my relationship with the Redskins Nation was actually just beginning.

WMAL at the time had the Redskin broadcasts. I was asked if I would be interested in coming back and broadcasting the games.

I can remember sitting in the booth watching Sonny standing on the sidelines. He rarely played, but when he did, he was still outstanding. George Allen favored his newly acquired quarterback Billy Kilmer. Sonny's injuries began to multiply, and in 1974, Jurgensen retired from the game. He went on to broadcast games for CBS.

By 1981, Sonny's contract with CBS had expired. I was now calling Redskin games with play-by-play man Frank Herzog, but with Sonny now available, WMAL's Andy Okershausen came up with an idea.

Andy knew that both Sonny and I had a great chemistry off camera and we had both worked in TV. He came to me and said that Sonny was a free agent. I told Andy, "I think Frank and I are pretty good, but I'll tell you this, if you bring Sonny in here, we will be great."

Like the chemistry we created as gridiron teammates, we became an instant hit with the fans, and a gameday tradition was conceived. People liked us so much that during the televised games they would turn the sound on their TV down and their radio up.

In 2005 Larry Michael took over the seat between Sonny and me. He was also our referee. When the Redskins defense wouldn't stand up to the challenge Sonny would just lay into me, and vice versa when the Redskins offensive was a three-and-out. I'd say it was Sonny's offense that couldn't do the job. It's not your normal broadcast, but it's a lot of fun.

Sonny will always be the best friend I ever had, and Sonny always says that I'm the brother he never had. That is an awesome feeling. From the first time we set foot on the football field, there was something special between us. We have been together for nearly 50 years as teammates, friends, and broadcast partners. The Redskins made us brothers. Brothers are family, and family is forever.

.

BIBLIOGRAPHY

Benson, Michael. *The Good, the Bad, and the Ugly New York Giants: Heart-pounding, Jaw-dropping, and Gut-wrenching Moments from New York Giants History*. Publisher: Triumph Books (September 15, 2007)

Bowden, Mark. *The Best Game Ever: Giants vs. Colts, 1958, and the Birth of the Modern NFL*. Publisher: Grove Press; First Trade Paper Edition (April 14, 2009)

Cavanaugh, Jack. *Giants Among Men: How Robustelli, Huff, Gifford, and the Giants Made New York a Football Town and Changed the NFL*. Publisher: Random House; 1 edition (October 7, 2008)

Corbett, Bernard M. and Baker, Jim. *The Most Memorable Games in Giants History: The Oral History of a Legendary Team*. Publisher: Bloomsbury USA (August 17, 2010)

Eisen, Michael. *Stadium Stories: New York Giants* (Stadium Stories Series). Publisher: Globe Pequot; 1st edition (August 1, 2005)

Eskenazi, Gerald. *There Were Giants in Those Days*. Publisher: Grosset and Dunlap (1976)

Freedman, Lew and Summerall, Pat. *New York Giants: The Complete Illustrated History*. Publisher: MVP Books; First edition (August 29, 2009)

Gifford, Frank and Richmond, Peter. *The Glory Game: How the 1958 NFL Championship Changed Football Forever*. Publisher: Harper Paperbacks; Reprint edition (November 3, 2009)

Goodman, Michael E. *The Story of the New York Giants (The NFL Today)*.

Publisher: Creative Education (July 15, 2009)

Herskowitz, Mickey. *The Golden Age of Pro Football.* Publisher: Taylor Pub (August 1990)

Huff, Sam and Shapiro, Leonard. *Tough Stuff.* Publisher: St Martins Press; 1 edition (September 1988)

Izenberg, Jerry. *New York Giants: Seventy-Five Years.* Publisher: Time Life (November 1999)

Maxymuk, John. *The 50 Greatest Plays in New York Giants Football History.* Publisher: Triumph Books (September 1, 2008)

Maxymuk, John. *Game Changers: The Greatest Plays in New York Giants History.* Publisher: Triumph Books (August 31, 2010)

O'Day, Joe. *Football's Furious Feud—Taylor vs. Huff—An Irresistible Force Meets An Immovable Object.* Publisher: Sports Quarterly Presents PROS Football '63 (no date given)

————. *PRO FOOTBALL, Brawn, Brains & Profits.* Publisher: Pro Football Magazine (November 30, 1959)

Pervin, Lawrence A. *Football's New York Giants: A History.* Publisher: McFarland (May 13, 2009)

Strasen, Marty. *New York Giants: Yesterday & Today.* Publisher: Publications International, Ltd. (August 4, 2009)

Tittle, Y.A. and Setting Clark, Kristine. *Nothing Comes Easy: My Life in Football.* Publisher: Triumph Books; 1 edition (September 1, 2009)

Whittingham, Richard. *What Giants They Were: New York Giants Greats Talk About Their Teams, Their Coaches, and the Times of Their Lives.* Publisher: Triumph Books (IL) (August 2001)

Whittingham Richard; Summerall, Pat; Hornung, Paul; and Ditka, Mike. *Sunday's Heroes: NFL Legends Talk About the Times of Their Lives.* Publisher: Triumph Books (IL) (September 2004)

NFL Films Top 100 Greatest Players. (#93—Sam Huff)
  NFL Films—2010
Biography—Sam Huff
  NFL Films—2002

Brothers of the Legacy—Keepers of the Flame: Huff/Jurgensen
   Washington Redskins Productions—2010
Linebackers Mic'd. Past and Present—Butkus, Taylor, and Huff
   NFL Films—2002
Time Magazine
"The Violent World of Sam Huff"
   November 30, 1959
Ranking All-Time New Orleans Saints Number One Draft Picks
   By Reggie Parquet / SAINTS @ New Orleans.com / April 2010
   www.neworleans.com/sports/saints/saints-news/376886-ranking-all-
   time-new-orleans-saints-number-one-draft-picks.html
   Accessed: 1-28-11

ABOUT THE AUTHORS

Sam Huff was a five-time Pro Bowl selection who spent his storied 13-year career with the New York Giants and the Washington Redskins. One of the first middle linebackers in NFL history, Huff bruised and battered his way to the 1956 NFL championship, while playing in six NFL Championship Games during his career. He was inducted into the College Football Hall of Fame in 1980 and the Pro Football Hall of Fame in 1982, and for more than 20 years he's been a color commentator on Redskins radio along with former teammate Sonny Jurgensen.

Dr. Kristine Setting Clark is a University of San Francisco graduate, author, and a feature writer for the San Francisco 49ers' and Dallas Cowboys' *Gameday* magazines. She has authored or coauthored six other books: *A Cowboy's Life; Undefeated, Untied, and Uninvited; St. Clair: I'll Take it Raw!; Legends of the Hall: The Fabulous Fifties; Nothing Comes Easy;* and *The Fire Within.* Dr. Clark resides in Northern California with her husband and has two grown children and two grandsons. Her grandson Justin is Hall of Fame member Bob St. Clair's godson.